the
New Apartment
book

the
New Ap

artment book

Michele Michael

Text with Wendy S. Israel
Photographs by Jeff McNamara

AURUM PRESS

For my mother, Ginny Grace,
and my grandparents, Horace and Isobel Gary,
with love

First published in Great Britain
1997 by Aurum Press Ltd,
25 Bedford Avenue, London WC1B 3AT

Copyright © 1996 by Michele Michael
Photographs copyright © 1996 by Jeff McNamara

Published by arrangement with Clarkson N. Potter, Inc., 201 East 50th Street, New York,
New York 10022.

Printed in China

Design by Helene Silverman

ISBN 1 85410 453 5

10 9 8 7 6 5 4 3 2 1

First Edition

acknowledgments

I am very happy to have the opportunity to thank everyone who took part in the production of this book. Foremost, I would like to thank my editor, Katie Workman, for her passion and dedication to this project. It was Katie's idea to do this book and I can't thank her enough for giving me the wonderful opportunity of bringing it to life.

Many, many thanks go to Jeff McNamara for his gorgeous photography and for always making a project fun to work on; Scott Jones for his help and always being on the lookout for great locations; Dina Scheffler for her patience in scheduling and rescheduling; Anne Dubuisson, my former agent, for her input, support, and guidance along the way; Elizabeth Kaplan, my new agent, for happily seeing the project through; Wendy Israel, for her clever way with words; Helene Silverman, who created a striking design for the book; Anne Foxley, who allowed me to photograph her own apartment and also led me to several of the fantastic locations in this book; Shawn Collins and Beth Boriss, my Paris shopping connection; Judy Langan and Alison Deyette, of Wellman, Inc., for their generous support; Marjorie Ford, of Schumacher, for all her help; and Anne Martin, of FSC Wallcoverings, and Katie Nelson, of Waverly, for letting me photograph their apartments and helping me enormously in the process.

I would also like to thank everyone at Clarkson Potter who worked so diligently on this book, including Jane Treuhaft, Erica Youngren, Mark McCauslin, and Joy Sikorski. My special thanks go to Lauren Shakely, Editorial Director, and Howard Klein, Art Director, for their constant support and enthusiasm throughout production.

I can't thank everyone enough who so generously allowed me to photograph their fantastic apartments: Anthony Baratta, Gary DiLuca and Melissa Makris, Michael Foster, Gary Freilich, Karen Gallen, Robert Gaul, Nicholas Kerno, Jessica Kimberly, Rita London and Eric Schurink, Darcey Miller, Carlos Mota, Craig Natiello, Laurie Sagalyn, Gayle Spannaus, and Lori Weitzner.

A very special thank you goes to Ginny Grace, my mother, who contributed her sewing skills to several projects in this book, and, most important, has always set a stellar example for me to follow. And to Patrick Moore, who spent countless hours building projects for the cause and spent many more hours keeping me amused through it all.

contents

Introduction	8
The Living Room	14
The Dining Area	66
The Kitchen	80
The Bedroom	96
The Bathroom	126
One-Room Living	138
Step-by-Step Projects	160
How-tos	178
Shopping Guide	193
Credits	203
Index	206

introduction

WHETHER you are moving into your very first apartment or your sixth, deciding how to decorate your new home is an exciting process, but sometimes a confusing one as well. You probably already have a collection of furniture and personal items, but most likely there are a few things you need, a few more you may simply want, and you are faced with the challenge of pulling all of this together into a single apartment that you feel proud to call home. This book will offer you a variety of inspiring design ideas, and help you think clearly about your needs, desires, and taste. Room by room, it's a practical and exciting do-it-yourself guide to decorating your space. To help make the process an easy one I've explained the most basic design principles to keep in mind, and provided guidelines for what materials and preparation you need to get started.

The real key to a successfully designed apartment is making it work for you. The pragmatic Le Corbusier believed that "the house is a machine for living." I agree;

however, besides being functional, it needs to be absolutely comfortable—both physically and mentally. As individuals we all have various needs, likes, and dislikes and it is very important to discern what these are before you get started. Most of us rent or buy an apartment that contains a number of rooms (or one room) that we then have to adapt to our own lifestyle. At this stage the important thing is to not let the space dictate to you how it's to be lived in; instead, you should decide what the best and most practical use of the space is for you.

Part of creating a comfortable environment is expressing your own personal style: surrounding yourself with things you love, things that hold memories and meaning to you. Learn to trust your own instincts while putting a room together; don't worry about buying things that "go together"; if you like it, most likely it will work in your apartment. Mixing styles and periods, colors and patterns, shapes and sizes will have far more interesting results than matching everything.

Decorating doesn't have to be expensive. Besides shopping flea markets, tag and estate sales, thrift shops, and junk stores, there are now a multitude of inexpensive home furnishings stores and mail-order catalogs to choose from. And don't forget the freebies you can find on the street, in a relative's attic, or even at the town dump.

Throughout the many wonderful apartments shown in this book I've included smart tips and how-to information to help you in your decorating projects. I've also focused on some decorating details for a close-up view of the role certain elements, such as color or pillows, can play in a room. In the back of the book you will find nine decorating projects that you can make yourself—just follow the step-by-step photographs and how-to instructions. Finally, there is a listing of great shopping sources for all your decorating needs. Let this book be the jumping-off point for your own creative brainstorms, try not to be too impatient (great homes don't get that way overnight), experiment (most changes are not permanent), and, most of all, enjoy yourself as you make your new apartment a unique and comfortable home.

DESIGN BASICS

Budget

At last, you've found the place that you can call home. But just because you used up the bulk of your bank account on the security deposit or a down payment doesn't mean you have to live in an empty nest. You just have to be smart. Even if you're short on time, money, or patience, you can still create a stylish living space, and have fun doing it.

Determining what you can afford to spend on decorating or redecorating your apartment is a very important first step. To do this, you'll need to decide how long you think you'll be living in this space. If it's a short-term rental (say, under three years), you'll want to spend almost all of your budget on furnishings that will move when you do. But if it's a long-term rental, or you own the apartment, put aside a portion of your budget for renovation or construction. Plan on spending money on rooms such as the kitchen or bath, where function is as important as looks and a potential buyer will appreciate an update. You don't have to spend a fortune to make a big impression. An inexpensive can of paint can revitalize walls and cabinets. Refinishing a wood floor yourself takes time but not a lot of money. Extra storage (built-in bookshelves, for example, or a well-organized closet) will certainly enhance the space while you live there, and may even add to the value of your home when you decide to sell.

Now think about furnishings. Decide which pieces are a must and how much you can afford to spend on each. Take time to shop around and compare prices. Invest in a good-quality sofa in a classic design, a bed and mattress, a bureau or other piece of furniture to hold your clothes if you don't have enough closet space, and a dining table and chairs if you have room. You can gradually and inexpensively fill in the rest—chairs, small tables, lamps, rugs, ottomans, pillows, and pictures—from flea markets

and tag sales, or you can even make them yourself. And it's easier than you think. For help, turn to page 202 for a list of flea markets around the world. And don't overlook secondhand stores, yard sales, your family's attic, or even pieces you already own, which may lend themselves to refinishing. Decorating doesn't have to be expensive. Remember, half the fun comes from finding the perfect piece—at a bargain price. Turn to page 202 for tips on bargain shopping.

Function

It's important to know exactly what your practical needs are before planning the design of your new space. Fortunately for the design novice, the basic layout and contents of a room, whether it's the kitchen, bedroom, living room, or bath, are generally predetermined, except if you live in a studio or loft. If that's the case, you'll need to define these areas yourself (see page 138 for more on one-room living).

Since needs vary, begin by asking yourself some basic questions: Do you work at home a lot? Maybe you should consider converting your dining room or a section of another room into a home office. Do you tend to eat dinner in front of the TV? Do you do a lot of entertaining? If so, what type? If you love to throw dinner parties and you don't have a dining room, consider giving over a portion of your living room to a dining space. Or for a more informal solution, scatter oversized pillows around the coffee table. Everyone has a unique style of living, and you shouldn't worry about tradition when it comes to laying out your space. What's important is that the design works for you. Both function and comfort can peacefully cohabit.

Creating comfort

More than the perfect sofa, more than the right shade of paint, even more than the silk damask drapes you splurged on, the key to a successful design of any apartment is comfort. From the moment you open the door to your apartment, you should feel, literally, at home.

But comfort isn't achieved merely with deep sofas and thick rugs (although physically comfortable furnishings are a good place to start). It also involves knowing exactly what makes you feel relaxed and happy. The right combination of light, color, and texture can work together to create a harmonious space. Things as simple as storage units to hide the clutter that drives you crazy, or a cozy reading chair with good light and a table nearby to rest your coffee mug, can also do the trick.

Style

Everyone has a unique personality. And since style is a reflection of your personality, you automatically have style. Now you need to learn how to express it in your new apartment. Begin by trusting yourself. Don't rush out and blindly follow the latest decorating trend if it doesn't feel right to "you." If you buy things you love, even when you're unsure if they go with everything else in the room, most often they will. Besides mixing, not matching, is much more interesting. Gone are the days of bedroom and dining suites. Feel free to combine styles and periods, which is what eclectic style is all about. You can always paint a table or recover a chair. You may end up making a few wrong purchases along the way, but who doesn't have an unworn pair of must-have shoes buried in the back of the closet?

Another way to put your personal stamp on a space is to personalize your new apartment with things that are precious to you; paintings you did in grade school, your grandmother's needlepoint pillows, sea glass you collected that foggy day at the beach. Beautiful things don't have to have a substantial price tag. Style is about combining things that have special meaning to you to create your own personal environment.

GETTING STARTED

Key to success

Whether you are moving into a new apartment or redecorating your current one, be well organized. A great way to begin is by choosing a binder or file folder that will hold all the information you need to help you make design and purchasing decisions. Make sure that it's compact and light enough to carry with you when you're out shopping, but still roomy enough to hold the following:

➤ A room-by-room floor plan (see below) as well as any other important measurements, such as the size of your sofa or bed, or the space in which you want to fit a potential piece of furniture. Most important, measure your doorways (you want to be sure your new purchases can fit through the door).

➤ Your decorating checklist (see below).

➤ Fabric swatches and paint chips.

➤ Inspirational pages clipped from magazines.

➤ Snapshots or Polaroids of your rooms and furnishings.

➤ A notebook, a pencil, and a tape measure.

So the next time you're searching for the perfect shade of blue paint at the hardware store or combing flea markets for just the right size dresser to fit between your windows, toss the folder in your bag and you'll have all the necessary information right at your fingertips.

The checklist

A decorating checklist will help you stay on track of what needs to be accomplished in your new apartment. Writing things down not only gives you an overview of your decorating plans, it forces you to think honestly about what you can accomplish. Be as realistic as possible when making out your list. Do not include things you cannot do or afford at this time. Each room should have its own checklist and budget. As you begin making purchases, deduct the costs from your bottom line so you can keep a running balance. Also fill in how you expect the room to function (say, a combination bedroom/home office or a living room/dining area). You'll also want to include any information on existing pieces or circumstances, such as

➤ accessories
➤ ceilings
➤ color palette
➤ floors
➤ furniture
➤ lighting
➤ storage
➤ walls
➤ window treatments

Floor plan

Creating a floor plan allows you determine how pieces will work in a room. It helps you work out a comfortable living arrangement and provides you with the immediate gratification of playing around with room arrangements before you actually move into your new place. Your floor plan also gives you an idea of what you need and where it may go, and encourages you to think carefully about the amount of space you have. If you work out a plan before you actually move in, you may find you don't want to move all your possessions with you. Moving is the perfect time to get rid of junk you no longer need or want. But always remember that one person's junk may be another person's treasure. Donate or give away anything you think can still be used or recycled. Or, if it's valuable, take it to a consignment shop. Otherwise, get rid of it!

To draw a floor plan, begin by making a rough sketch of your room. Include windows, doorways, fireplaces, built-ins, radiators, and anything else that affects the layout of your room. Then take your tape measure and mark the length of your walls, and the width of windows and doorways. To make an accurately scaled plan, which will give you the exact proportions of your room, you'll need to convert the real measurements into smaller measurements that will fit on your paper. The best way to do this is to use a scale of 1 foot equals ¼ inch. For example, if your room is 20 feet by 8 feet, your drawing will be 5 inches by 2 inches. Using graph paper will make the process easier. Do the same conversion with your furniture and draw it on a separate piece of graph paper. Cut the pieces out and play around with them on your floor plan to create room settings. When you arrive at an arrangement you like, glue the pieces down and use this as your guide.

Tools of the trade

In order to tackle almost any do-it-yourself decorating project, you will need to have some very basic tools and equipment on hand. You don't have to buy all your tools at once; purchase them as you need them. By buying the best quality you can afford and taking care of them, you ensure that your tools will last you a lifetime. Keep your tools organized, whether they're stored in a shoe box, a tool kit, or a heavy-duty canvas tote. When it comes time to do a project, you will always know exactly where they are.

BASIC TOOL KIT

glue gun and glue sticks
hammer
handsaw
jigsaw
level
metal ruler
screwdrivers in various sizes
Phillips-head screwdriver
variable-speed power drill, and bits for wood
   and masonry
putty knife
scissors
staple gun
T square
tape measure
utility knife

Other essentials

electrical tape
masking tape
nails
paintbrushes
picture hooks
screws
wall anchors
wood glue
wood putty

Equipment to Have on Hand or Accessible

five-foot folding ladder
iron and ironing board
sewing machine

the
living
room

The living room is aptly named. After all, it's where you do all your living. Unless you live in a palatial apartment with many rooms, you need to make your living room work extra hard for you. The challenge lies in creating a space that's functional, comfortable, and personal.

Thankfully, today's living room is no longer an untouched monument to high design or a place reserved for polite conversation. It's where you'll throw large, boisterous cocktail parties and quiet intimate dinners. You'll need to find a niche for your TV, VCR, CD player, and maybe a computer. You'll also want a corner to relax with a magazine, and a place to put up the inevitable overnight visitor. And this room is also a gallery where you can display your collections—of photos, paintings, pottery, whatever—and stash things away in secret storage areas. But most of all, your living room is the place to experiment and have fun with your own sense of style.

A splash of color

A jolt of chartreuse instantly adds color and focus to a mostly monochromatic apartment. The remaining three walls, which were kept a pristine white, and industrial carpet in charcoal black provide an understated background.

Eclectic accessories fill the room. The harlequin lamp is an authentic fifties find. The striking oversized print above the sofa was purchased at a flea market and shows a view of the east side of Manhattan (the tall building in front is the United Nations).

The undulating sofa is encased in faux leopard. Don't be afraid to take a walk on the wild side with animal prints. Treat them as you would any pattern and use them judiciously. The chrome lounge chair is upholstered in black leather and an overscaled houndstooth fabric (combining leather with a less expensive fabric not only holds down costs, it looks more exciting than solid leather). A round chair is covered in a comfortable quilted fabric that picks up the green of the wall. Remember when choosing fabric that texture is as important as color. The ottoman here is covered in shiny white vinyl. (And vinyl's practical, too. Scuff marks wipe off with a quick spritz of window cleaner.)

Right, the chartreuse of one wall in this living room instantly focuses your eye on the vintage photograph of New York City.

Big-city glamour

At first glance, the elegant furnishings of this prewar apartment seem custom-made for this room. In fact, most of the furniture was originally chosen for a traditional English country look. But with a few simple tricks, it was transformed to fit into this more glamorous, urban setting. Don't stick yourself with a style that you'll outgrow—or grow tired of—just because you already own a bunch of pieces from a particular period. The best investments, and the furniture that you will enjoy the most, are the pieces that can evolve with your changing tastes.

Here, furniture that was previously covered in blue-and-pink mattress ticking was reupholstered and slipcovered in saturated shades of red and gold. The rich-looking fabrics (a combination of cut velvets, velvet, and damask) were purchased at discount fabric stores. Reupholstering large pieces of furniture is difficult to do yourself and should be done by a professional. However, since it can be costly, you should take the time to shop around for the best price, and don't be afraid to negotiate, particularly if you are planning on reupholstering two or more pieces at one time. A cheaper alternative to reupholstering is slipcovering. Slipcovers can be purchased ready-made, sewn yourself, or custom-made. Cheaper still, and easiest of all, is to simply drape a sheet, blanket, or other piece of fabric over the piece and tuck it in so that the shape of the furniture is defined. A word of caution: If material is badly damaged, stuffing is loose, or springs are sticking out, you're better off opting for reupholstery.

The newly recovered furniture was arranged in the room so that two distinct seating areas were created. Flanking the fireplace, whose beautifully carved mantel naturally draws people in, is the main gathering area. Two armchairs face each other, while the sofa sits at a slight angle, so the arrangement doesn't look too uptight. Here, a group of people can sit close enough for conversation, drinks, or an informal meal. The tufted ottoman does triple duty as a footrest, stool, and small occasional table—a tole tray on top provides a stable surface. A contemporary dhurrie rug underfoot subtly defines the area's perimeters.

Over by the windows is a second, more intimate sitting area with an Empire daybed. A daybed or chaise may sound like an old-fashioned, frivolous purchase. But not only is it an ideal spot for reading, it can also be pressed into service as a comfortable guest bed if you don't have a spare bedroom or fold-out couch.

smart tip

If you like the look of black-and-white photos, but can't afford their steep price tag, buy an art book of your favorite photographer's work or genre. Frame pages in inexpensive black metal or wood frames with white matting.

When you're lucky enough to have a space that has strong lines—such as the French windows in this living room, above—play them up. Here, the horizontal lines of the daybed provide a strong contrast to the windows. When setting up space, don't overlook practicalities, opposite. A mere arm's length away from the daybed, an old plant stand serves as a magazine holder. Close by is a small table that doubles as a nightstand when guests stay over.

Left, in an oversized living room, a congregation of upholstered furniture is arranged to encourage conversation in front of the fireplace. A chaise is set up near the windows for more privacy. Think of the mantel as a temporary exhibition space that is constantly changing. Here, faux tortoise tole (decorative painted metalware) cachepots hold bright red tulips that frame a black-and-white photo. In front stand two candlesticks with beaded shades.

Colorful additions

To play up the colorful elements in this living room, the walls, floor, and window treatments were intentionally kept a neutral off-white. Opting for eye-popping furnishings that will move with you, rather than spending time and money changing the color of the walls, is also a good idea if you're going to be living in the apartment for only a short period of time.

With the exception of the sofa and the coffee table, all the pieces here were unearthed at flea markets and tag sales. The pair of forties armchairs were purchased at the Brimfield flea and antique market in Massachusetts, one of the largest in the country. At a mere $70 for the pair, you can afford to indulge in a few yards of expensive fabric (in this case, lipstick-red velvet) and professional reupholstering, and still feel as if you're getting a bargain.

The ottoman was a lucky street find, transformed into a jaunty striped beauty. Here's an example of an easy do-it-yourself recovering accomplished with the help of a staple gun, batting, and some burlap and velvet fabric. While shopping, strolling, or driving, keep your eyes open for upholstered pieces with good lines; don't be distracted by ugly fabrics. Refurbishing may easily be cheaper than buying a new piece.

A trio of framed prints is suspended on a three-paneled screen cut with a fleur-de-lis silhouette on top of each panel. See page 187 for instructions. Each section is painted a different color, inspired by the colors in the striped fabric on the ottoman and throw pillow in front. Besides being beautiful, and an interesting place to hang pictures, the screen shields ugly storage boxes from view. The Victorian parlor chair was scavenged curbside and recovered in a deep Bordeaux velvet.

A collection of green-hued Arts and Crafts pottery is an unexpected alternative to framed pictures and gives dimension to flat walls. Each vessel sits on its own wooden box shelf (see page 174 for instructions). The box shelves are painted off-white to blend into the wall, and yet provide a slight sense of depth as well. This growing collection of pottery overflows onto a wooden dresser, which is also used to store towels and linens.

Opposite, an old family clock has the place of honor on the mantel, the spot it's occupied for generations in many different homes. Above, Arts and Crafts pottery is no longer the bargain it used to be. If you're just beginning to collect, search out unmarked pieces, which are considerably cheaper. The various heights of this all-green grouping keep things from looking dull. Overleaf, left, in this apartment, a neutral background allows the colorful furnishings to stand out. A seating area was created by two red chairs that cozy up to an oversized rolled-arm sofa. A wonderful way to introduce color quickly and cheaply into an apartment is with flowers. Overleaf, right, a fleur-de-lis screen painted in a variety of saturated colors does double duty as a display for photographs and a shield for storage.

smart tip

When displaying "objets d'art," remember there's strength in numbers. Group pieces by size, shape, color, or theme.

color

Color has the distinct ability to transform a room in many wonderful ways. It has the power to camouflage flaws, give focus to a room, and affect your mood. ■ Pale neutrals, or various shades of the same color, can create a harmonious atmosphere. Conversely, complementary colors (opposites on the color wheel such as green and red) create a stimulating setting. Warm colors, such as orange, yellow, or red, tend to advance in a room, providing a sense of intimacy or coziness. Cool colors—blue and green—can soothe and calm while giving a greater sense of space. And white is obviously the noncolor of choice for a crisp, clean look, but don't choose a white too quickly—there are many different shades, ranging from very cool to warmer, creamier tones. ■ Paint can be one of the least expensive ways to introduce color into a room—on walls, ceilings, trim, floors, doors, and furniture. Other low-cost ways to add a splash of color are with accessories: pillows, throws, lamp shades, a vase filled with flowers, or a bowl filled with fresh fruit. ■ Use colors you love most, remembering that you can continually adjust your palette. And if you are attracted to a variety of palettes, you can express yourself differently in two separate rooms.

Playing with tradition

A combination of antiques, contemporary art, and street-finds give this room a look of easy-going sophistication. A palette of neutral colors—white, cream, and beige—keeps things light and airy in an apartment that doesn't get much natural sun. Choosing sisal carpeting and linen fabrics also keeps things clean and simple.

Whimsical objects provide an amusing touch. A plaster arm protruding from the wall grasps a candle; an ordinary blackboard is an ever-changing canvas. Chalk is left out on the coffee table so guests can freely express themselves. The coffee table itself is an old wooden warehouse pallet rescued from the city street. Piles of books on top provide yet another surface for displaying objects. A rusted machine part, resting on the floor, becomes a sculptural item. The result is a room that looks lived-in and full of personal expression.

Above, plaids, checks, and stripes all freely cohabit in this living room, yet the room has an overwhelming feeling of calm. The secret? The colors are all muted. Opposite, art should intrigue as well as stimulate. This large photograph above the chair shows the view looking up at the sky through an arched stone formation. A nearby group of books acts as a plant stand for a red amaryllis. Place a saucer under the pot to protect book covers.

Don't shy away from using oversized art in a small room. But for the sake of balance, hang works on more than one wall.

smart tip

The art of living

This tiny apartment appears much larger than it actually is due to the clever use of mirrors, art, and small-scale furnishings. To begin, two mirrors were installed opposite the entrance and framed with molding that echoes molding found in the rest of the apartment. Framed portraits were hung over the mirrors to playfully confuse the boundaries of the room.

Many of the furnishings in this living room were castoffs from friends and relatives. Don't be afraid to express interest in potential giveaways when friends are redecorating their places—think of it as recycling. A simple admiring comment could send you home with a new chair or a bust of Caesar!

Here, an armless love seat and wing chair were slipcovered in white duckcloth, an inexpensive and easy-to-care-for material that you can toss in the washing machine. Less permanent than reupholstering, slipcovering allows you to easily change the decor of a room. Try using darker, heavier fabrics in winter; lighter ones in summer. Or simply change them when you want a new look.

A sisal rug is an inexpensive way to hide an unattractive wood floor. Here, an old zebra rug was layered on top. The black-and-white motif is maintained throughout the apartment by accessories such as a checkered throw on the sofa and the striped candlesticks on the coffee table. The table itself was cleverly made by stacking books from a thrift store (notice they're all copies of the same book) and topping them with a ¾-inch-thick piece of glass. Simply adding or subtracting more books changes the height. (Be careful not to use valuable books for this—the weight of the glass can ruin bindings.) A vintage Louis Vuitton trunk salvaged from a neighbor becomes a side table and provides hidden storage space, truly a boon in a very small apartment.

Wall space in this petite pad is maximized within a square inch. Prints are hung over doors in addition to being layered over mirrors. (If you don't want to leave holes behind, use brass or nickel hangers that go over the top of the door, or hang from picture molding.) Unusual framed Japanese woodblock prints, which had been sent as invitations, hang in the entryway. Although most people don't receive invitations this extravagant, there are many other bits of ephemera that are worthy of art treatment. Try programs from a favorite play, sheet music, magazine jackets (especially those that commemorate a special event), vintage record album covers, and so on.

smart tip

In a room with a lot of symmetry try to keep it from becoming too staid by placing something on an angle, such as the zebra rug in this room.

Opposite, although there seems to be a lot going on in this room, it's actually quite organized. Books and magazines are stacked like columns on chairs and under tables; lighting is conveniently set up where you need it. An angled zebra rug seems to lead guests directly to the seating area.

Left, instead of filling a wall with one giant picture, try multiples. These woodblocks were framed and hung on the wall in groups of three. (When in doubt, arrange things in bunches of three. For some reason, trios seem to work best.) Above, a vintage Louis Vuitton chest not only looks sophisticated, it also provides storage (and who doesn't need an extra drawer or closet?). Keep things inside that are used infrequently, such as out-of-season clothes, so you can use the top as an extra table or desk. A well-placed lamp spotlights artwork.

A stylish mix

You love to entertain, but your apartment doesn't have a spare ballroom. Plus, you still need some space to spread out and take care of paperwork. This living room shows how to solve both these problems.

First, the room is divided by a sisal rug into a sitting area and a dining room. But many of the furnishings have dual roles. An Asian console (snatched up at a going-out-of-business sale) acts as both a storage cabinet and a sideboard; the ottoman serves as a footrest, extra seat, or serving piece; the dining table also functions as a desk or a library table when a piece of glass is placed over the tablecloth. This cloth is made of burlap edged in a jute fringe (see instructions on page 178). Burlap is a great, inexpensive alternative to linen, and you still get a wonderful textured look.

At night, the table sparkles due to a combination of glass, silver, and candlelight. The dinner plates were hand-painted. Check your Yellow Pages for local ceramic shops. Often they carry bisqueware that is ready to be glazed. You decorate the pieces and they fire them.

Throughout the room, candles create a magnificent glow. Don't be stingy—buy more than you think you'll need. These are all the same shape, but vary in height to create different levels of light. You can create different looks by combining different sizes, shapes, colors, or a blend of all three.

Your living room often has to function as your dining room as well. When entertaining a group, set up your table within close distance of the sitting area so you can take advantage of additional seating. If the party is less formal, you might just want to use the coffee table and sit around it on the sofa, chairs, and floor.

When setting a table for a dinner party, keep flower arrangements small and low. Nothing is worse than not being able to see the person across from you. An easy solution: Use glass tumblers to hold small bouquets.

Above right, organize a large collection by grouping similar pieces in an artful still life. Use this same method when storing items, such as magazines or books, to keep clutter at bay. **Opposite,** put your finest effort forward when setting a table. You don't need to own cut-lead crystal and fine bone china to make things sparkle. Combining crisp whites, clear glass, and shiny silver in your tableware can add brilliance to your table. **Right,** your own hand-painted bisqueware personalizes your table with a note of whimsy.

Elegantly eclectic

Perseverance pays off in this apartment—everything was purchased at flea markets. The only rule: Buy only what you absolutely love and only what you need. If you find a piece you like more than the one you already own, trade the old one in or give it to a friend in need. Or, if it's valuable, sell it through a consignment shop.

Forget anything you might have heard about matching furniture. Don't be afraid to mix different styles and periods. When you buy what you love, everything will almost always end up working together. For example, a Victorian velvet sofa and fifties faux-leopard-covered chairs work just fine with a Deco iron console and side tables. What they all share: beautiful, graceful lines. What makes it all work isn't always apparent. But remember, it's your style at play here.

Even the fabrics are flea market finds. Vintage forties drapes needed only a little shortening to fit these windows. Looped trim from a fabric shop was added along the sides and at the bottom. Keep notes of room and window measurements in your wallet for easy reference—sometimes you'll happen upon a find, and you don't want to be caught unprepared.

The interior of this apartment seems bathed in a golden glow thanks to the pale yellow glazed walls (see instructions on page 179). Instead of merely applying paint to the walls, the surface was ragged with glaze over a base coat. Although this technique takes more time than applying a solid color, it's well worth the extra effort.

Right, this living room was created with a collection of flea market finds, patiently put together over several years. Lineage and pedigree were not a consideration here. Instead, curvy lines and delicate framework are the common bonds.

Play around when setting out your artwork, right. You may come up with some unlikely scenarios. Here, the lines of an upholstered chair share the same curves as the figures in the portraits. Above, build your own table for a very personal statement, such as this one made from two columns and a sheet of glass. In front is a velvet sofa draped with a fringed piano shawl.

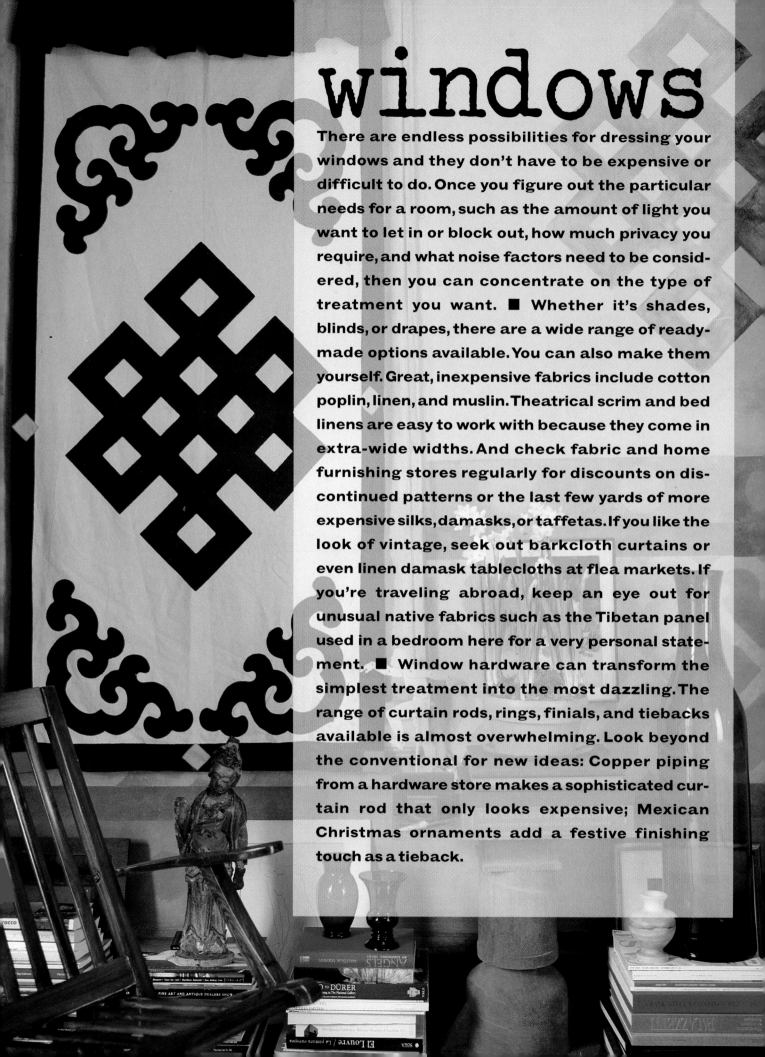

windows

There are endless possibilities for dressing your windows and they don't have to be expensive or difficult to do. Once you figure out the particular needs for a room, such as the amount of light you want to let in or block out, how much privacy you require, and what noise factors need to be considered, then you can concentrate on the type of treatment you want. ■ Whether it's shades, blinds, or drapes, there are a wide range of ready-made options available. You can also make them yourself. Great, inexpensive fabrics include cotton poplin, linen, and muslin. Theatrical scrim and bed linens are easy to work with because they come in extra-wide widths. And check fabric and home furnishing stores regularly for discounts on discontinued patterns or the last few yards of more expensive silks, damasks, or taffetas. If you like the look of vintage, seek out barkcloth curtains or even linen damask tablecloths at flea markets. If you're traveling abroad, keep an eye out for unusual native fabrics such as the Tibetan panel used in a bedroom here for a very personal statement. ■ Window hardware can transform the simplest treatment into the most dazzling. The range of curtain rods, rings, finials, and tiebacks available is almost overwhelming. Look beyond the conventional for new ideas: Copper piping from a hardware store makes a sophisticated curtain rod that only looks expensive; Mexican Christmas ornaments add a festive finishing touch as a tieback.

A calm oasis

Cool blues and greens in this apartment create a tranquil oasis of elegance amid the hustle and bustle of city life outside. A textured, but soft, seagrass rug covers the floor; the sofa is covered with velvet pillows made from vintage fabrics and trim.

To accentuate the height of the room, curtains are hung from an iron rod close to the ceiling. The draped console table actually conceals secret extra storage: Two wire filing drawers stand side by side topped with a piece of plywood. Draping floor-length tablecloths over the top disguises the whole unit.

A pair of Chippendale chairs were purchased at a tag sale and skirted with Irish linen in modest length (see how-to instructions on page 185). Chartreuse satin bows secure the seat covers. The gold-colored frames above the chairs were purchased at Portobello, the year-round flea market in London. They surround nineteenth-century handwritten letters covered with wax seals, also flea-market finds. Old family letters, documents, invitations, and announcements can also be elegantly displayed this way.

In this apartment, the sofa sits in perfect balance between two oversized windows. The velvet pillows lay in contrast with the silk drapes, sea grass rug, and zebra-covered footstool.

One of the biggest investments in a new apartment is a sofa—buy the best one you can afford. The higher the quality, the longer you will own it.

smart tip

Slipcovers are a great way to change the style or character of a piece of furniture. Linen ruffled skirts can give traditional chairs a romantic twist.

Right, you would never guess that this beautifully dressed table (top) hides wire basket files underneath its pale green and white overlay (bottom). Opposite, a pair of Chippendale chairs are for sitting or admiring.

The illustrated room

This richly patterned apartment is an homage to travel as well as ingenuity. Trips to London and Paris inspired the apartment's sensibility, but a limited budget dictated the ultimate purchasing decisions. For instance, inspired by a postcard from London's Victoria and Albert Museum, a talented friend painted the zebra now hanging above the sofa. If you're not in a position to ask an artist friend to execute a painting, you might look into the many beautiful museum exhibit posters available, including those of older vintage.

Bargains aren't solely the province of flea markets. Often mass-market or department stores can yield rich bounty. The slipper chairs and ottoman in this room were purchased new at a department store. The wooden cabinets with glass-front doors are mass-produced and easily available at discount stores. These cabinets were customized by stenciling the exteriors with black paint and covering the inside of the glass doors with inexpensive lining fabric. They are now a far cry from the original nondescript pieces.

The living room drapes are sewn from ordinary bed sheets. The needlepoint fabric with bullion fringe that makes up part of the valance was purchased at the Clignancourt flea market in Paris, but it wasn't quite wide enough for the windows. A piece of border fabric, attached so that the stripes are at a 45 degree angle, came to the rescue.

Left, let your travels (or imagination) inspire your decor. This sitting area carries memories of Europe, Africa, and the Far East in its fabric, art, and accessories. Above right, mix and match a variety of patterns for a one-of-a-kind look. Right, don't be afraid to let a simple piece, such as this celadon vase, stand on its own.

Pillows can be quite expensive, yet they are one of the easiest things to make (see pages 173, 188, and 189). Look at flea markets for interesting pieces of fabric but carefully check their condition. If a piece is damaged, it may continue to deteriorate, especially if you put pressure on it.

Above, even up close, you'd never know that the cabinets are inexpensive mass-market pieces from a discount store, with some creative touches added. The hand-stenciled pattern on the sides was inspired by the design on the wall. Right, pattern on top of pattern creates a rich environment.

A new take on tradition

If your tastes lean toward cozy English or another more traditional period, but you live in a modern postwar building, don't despair. Instead, try mixing soft fabrics, deep colors, and patterns. The result is a fresher, more modern take on tradition. But don't go overboard with too much pattern; you want your decor to enhance, not fight, your space.

Since the living room in this high-rise building has a knockout view, a soft gauzy window treatment was opted for, which still gives a glimpse of the city and the river. Curtains are suspended from the ceiling with hooks to maximize the standard ceiling height and conceal unattractive aluminum window frames.

To add architectural interest to this plain white box of a room, a shelf made from cornice molding was attached to the wall. The extra-wide surface provides plenty of room to display photos and even small collectibles such as candles or miniature vases.

Tactile fabrics that soften hard edges and feel sensuous, too, were used throughout the living room. A crushed velvet tablecloth (a yard of fabric with unfinished edges) has been tossed over a pine coffee table while it awaits refinishing. The sleeper sofa is upholstered in a rich red chenille; the chair is covered in a pale olive crushed velvet. Scraps of leftover velvet were turned into a patchwork throw pillow, which also adds a bit of pattern to a solid-colored piece of furniture (see page 173 for instructions). The lush solid-color fabrics allow the richly patterned rug to take center stage, while the colors of the furniture underline some of the accent colors in the pattern.

Right, jewel-toned furnishings seem even more brilliant set off by white walls and curtains. Above, a windowsill is lined with votive candles and olive oil bottles-cum-vases, whose shapes are reminiscent of the city's skyscrapers.

Save empty glass water, olive oil, vinegar, and liqueurs bottles and soak the labels off. Their beautiful shapes and colors make wonderful, impromptu vases.

smart tip

Above, personal mementos are displayed throughout this living room. Above and below right, a striped tablecloth cleverly conceals storage of items waiting for use.

Objects of desire

Objects, both found and purchased, play an important role in the living room of this pre-war apartment. Furniture is kept simple and forms the perfect backdrop to display quirky finds. Above the working fireplace and built-in bookshelves, an antique grain shovel and hand-carved pitchfork take center stage. On the mantel, bells from Thailand stand on their own. Valuable objects as well as sentimental ones such as glass bottles, pebbles, and seashells are all displayed with the same loving care.

Artwork by friends and family is also scattered throughout the apartment. Brightly painted watercolors resting on windowsills provide a sunny view year-round.

A table fashioned from two sawhorses and a wooden board is covered with a tablecloth and fastened with ribbon ties for easy access to woven storage baskets underneath.

smart tip

Terra-cotta pots (with no holes in the bottom) make beautiful vases reminiscent of Italian pottery.

High drama

Instantly add drama to a room by painting it a bold color such as deep cobalt blue. Intense color can also make a palatial, high-ceiling room seem more intimate. The trim in this living room was painted a metallic gold for an elegant touch.

Oversized windows were treated like canvases. Pagoda-inspired valences were cut from plywood and painted a complementary Chinese red (see page 183). The crisp, pin-striped curtain panels are actually twin-sized sheets hung from a tension rod that runs through the hem of the sheets—easy, inexpensive, and no sewing is necessary! And if they're too long, consider letting them puddle gently on the floor.

Underneath, the 1930's sofa had seen better days, but draped in pools of velvet, it now fits in with the luxurious setting. The wood floors were in good condition, so they were left bare.

On the mantel, empty grappa bottles, which come in beautiful, fluid shapes, hold candles and a single orchid. Lit by candle-light, the room becomes even more dramatic and romantic.

Opposite, everyday objects and musical instruments become a still life in front and on top of the beautifully carved marble fireplace. Above left, white objects take on an extra luminosity juxtaposed against a rich cobalt-blue wall.

smart tip

When accessorizing a piece that is itself ornamental (for example, this mantel), use simple objects that enhance instead of compete with the structure's shape.

Paint is one of the easiest and cheapest ways to personalize a space. Before purchasing enough paint to do your room, buy a quart for testing. Brush a big patch on one wall and live with it for a few days, making sure that you view it in natural and incandescent light or your lighting of choice, whatever that may be. You'll be surprised how much the color will change. If you want to adjust the color, you'll find that out before you've painted the entire area and invested in a lot of paint.

Create a dramatic sitting area with deep, saturated color. Crisp pin-striped drapes (made cheaply and easily from bed sheets) allow plenty of light to filter through.

texture

When you're designing a room, there's more to consider than furnishings and color. Texture, which combines the visual experience with the tactile, gives a room strength of character and depth. It can create warmth or coolness. Combining textures is key to balancing your space and gives your rooms the finishing touch. ■ If you have many smoothly finished furnishings—a glass coffee table, a leather-covered chair, a polished wood floor—introduce some rough surfaces. A nubby sisal rug can be spread underfoot. A wicker chair can be placed nearby, or a chenille throw tossed over your sofa. Think smooth and rough, soft and hard—contrasts. ■ The same principles apply to your accessories. Instead of placing shiny pieces near other bright things, opt for the opposite. A silver bowl and a biscuit jar sit inside an old wooden tray, whose peeling paint is in sharp contrast to the mirrored surfaces. An old ceramic container sits on contemporary steel shelving. Your rooms will become far more interesting when textures are mixed, not matched.

Simply chic

This could be a farmhouse in the south of France or a flat in London, yet it happens to be a fifth-floor walk-up apartment in Manhattan. The chic, casual elegance is achieved by combining beautiful materials without overdoing it.

Begin by covering surfaces in sunny hues. Here, pale yellow walls are topped with a wide gray acanthus wallpaper border. (Border prints are a fast and cheap way to add subtle detailing to a room, and less of a commitment than wallpaper.) Floors are painted white to brighten the room and camouflage worn floorboards. The sofa is slipcovered in a fabric reminiscent of Marseilles coverlets and finished at the corners with wide satin bows laced through grommets.

The casual feel is carried throughout by the choice of accessories: The simple, gold framed cherub is not a print—it's a piece of fabric. A galvanized bucket holds Queen Anne's lace. The chair, a junk store find, was professionally recovered in a floral medallion fabric. The yellow-and-white checkerboard pillows are trimmed with a ruffle—one in white, the other in yellow (see instructions on page 189). The rectangular pillow is half white and half yellow, with the seam running down the center with its ruffle contrasting on either side.

Opposite, painting the floor white brightens up a tiny living room and makes it seem larger than it actually is. Covering the large roll-arm sofa in white and the chair in a pale yellow pattern keeps things light. Above left, a wide satin bow embellishes each corner of the sofa. Left, everyday objects can make artful accessories. Here, a galvanized tin bucket holds wildflowers and a toast rack turns into a photo display.

Picture-perfect

Often the best design decisions happen purely by chance. While stripping layers of paint from the wooden fireplace mantle, the owners found that they preferred the distressed look and decided to leave it as is. The lesson: Keep an open mind when you're putting rooms together and don't be afraid to stray from your original plans.

The rustic fireplace in this living room is particularly striking contrasted against serene vanilla walls and a collection of stark black-and-white prints.

Frames stand on two gallery shelves (see page 161 for instructions) that run the length of one wall, so they can be rearranged at will. Several of the mattes here are covered in green velvet (see page 176 for instructions). You can use any kind of fabric or even paper to add personality to plain store-bought mattes. Be creative when putting together mattes, frames, and images.

Blend rustic touches in among finer furnishings to loosen things up. In this living room a distressed wooden mantel, a Shaker coffee table, a wrought-iron sconce, and a metal side table sit alongside a classic wing chair and a leather sofa. Two picture rails running alongside the length of the wall support an ever-changing parade of prints.

smart tip

Since custom framing can often be expensive, buy unfinished frames and paint them. Secure prints to matte boards with black photo corners instead of cutting them to size.

the
dining
area

Considering how complicated and busy life is today, we often
need to reinvent traditional living spaces. Case in point: the dining
room. Whether you're married or single, with or without children,
you probably find yourself all too often eating on the run or in
front of the TV. Depending on your lifestyle, you may not need—
or have room for—a formal dining area, but you still want a place
to enjoy a meal in comfort.

To get the most out of your space, consider the obvious as well
as the not so obvious. Use a part of your kitchen if it's large enough.
Or set up a drop-leaf table in an extra-wide hallway. A round table
works well in a foyer since it's easy to get around it. And, of course,
you can set aside a corner of your living room, where your dining
table can pinch-hit as a desk. A coffee table is probably the most
spontaneous eating area. Throw big, fluffy pillows around it for a
casual dinner party.

If you can't keep a table out permanently, stash a folding card
table in the closet or under your bed. With a pretty tablecloth
thrown over it, no one will ever know what lurks underneath.

Repeat performance

A dining room can be formal without relying on an expensive set of furniture. In this comfortably traditional yet still modern dining room, color and pattern were all that was needed to create the desired effect.

To begin, a small-scale harlequin-print wallpaper in the palest taupe and white covers the walls. Scattered randomly throughout the decorative paper are pearlescent diamonds that, when hit with light, make the room come alive. New chairs were upholstered in a similar pattern, but the diamonds are slightly larger and deeper in tone. An unattractive table is covered with a heavyweight tablecloth in natural linen. Hugging the ceiling, baseboards, doorway, and windows is a narrow scroll-pattern border paper, which gives the illusion of more expensive wood molding.

Dark woods, such as the 1940s cabinet, look extra rich in this pale setting. The cabinet was actually a serendipitous acquisition, left behind by a previous tenant. Now it conveniently stores dishes, glassware, and table linens, as well as the stereo.

Inexpensive dashes of color give this room a playful spirit. Each candle in the iron chandelier is a different luscious fruit color; the table centerpiece is a truffle compote filled with oranges, lemons, limes, and grapefruits; an Arts and Crafts vase overflows with tulips.

smart tip

Don't use scented candles in the dining area. The sweet smell can ruin a meal.

Previous page, a formal dining room in shades of taupe and white has its less traditional moments: Floorboards are painted white, a candelabra rests on the floor, and a chandelier holds a variety of colored candles. Above, drapes are sewn from white linen and appliquéd with natural linen cut in an overscaled zigzag pattern (see sewing instructions on page 170). The drapes are tied with white satin bows to a black wrought-iron curtain rod, which has spear finials. Right, an edible centerpiece overflows onto the table.

Pattern to dine for

A variety of pattern and color manages to work well together in this small dining area. The secret is to temper strong patterns with soft colors—and vice versa. The subtle shades of blue and yellow in the geometric designs on the wall, for example, hold their own against the striking Chinese red upholstered chairs.

No surface is left untouched in this room. Instead of a rug, which can trap crumbs, floorboards were stripped and stained with a multitude of stripes. Even the surface of the table (a drafting board when not being used for eating) has yellow and red stripes, which make a tablecloth or place mats strictly optional.

smart tip Lay out an inexpensive terracotta floor in a special pattern such as a basketweave or herringbone for a rich look at no more cost than plain terracotta tiles. If you fall in love with a high-price tile, splurge on just a few pieces and carefully integrate them into the pattern. You'll get a beautiful look for a lot less money.

The dining nook

The far end of a kitchen is transformed into an intimate dining area using the same luxe treatment as if it were a grand ballroom. But the room is as functional as it is beautiful. Walls are glazed a deep crimson, which makes them look richer than mere paint, but costs the same. A bamboo chair (which you can easily find in import shops) sits opposite a built-in banquette-for-two, whose skirt conceals extra storage space. (Use plastic or wooden bins that slide or roll out for easy access.) Discreetly tucked underneath the glass-top table is a wire recycling bin for newspapers. Flattering light emanates from the table lamp and candles set in the entrance arch.

Left, beyond a brick archway lies an intimate dining area that conceals extra storage space. Above, pattern as well as color can create a rich dining experience. This dining room has both—in just the right doses.

flowers

Although they may seem like an indulgence, flowers can be one of the cheapest ways to make your apartment come alive. And what could be more pleasant than coming home to a fresh bouquet or a beautiful flowering plant? ■ To keep down costs, buy whichever flowers are in season. And don't pay extra for arrangements in fancy holders. Instead, start your own collection. Look for vases, pitchers, terra-cotta pots, buckets, or out-of-the-ordinary containers such as teacups, glasses, and bowls at flea markets and tag sales. Don't worry if they have small chips, cracks, or brown water marks inside; it's the flowers you'll be looking at. Recycle beautiful olive oil and vinegar bottles as well as coffee tins (espresso brands, especially from Europe, come in wonderful colors), cleaning them thoroughly before putting flowers in them. When shopping for flowers, opt for quality over quantity. A single, perfect orchid is worth a dozen wilted roses. And get rid of the baby's breath and asparagus fern that the florist usually throws in—it only cheapens the arrangement! ■ Keep a variety of containers on hand in many shapes and sizes to accommodate different species: The heavy blooms of peonies and lilacs look best in a widemouthed pitcher; a bunch of wildflowers is right at home in an old glass mason jar. Plan around with different arrangements: Feature a few tulips in a narrow vase, mass daisies in a pail, try groups of single types of flowers, or mix colors and variety of blooms. Always trim the bottom of your flowers with a knife and remove any leaves that will be submerged before placing them in water. Remove dead flowers from bouquets and be sure to change your water daily to prolong the life of the blooms.

Restaurant style

Above, a cozy dining table contains all the elements of the best corner table in an Italian trattoria: snowy white linens, soft candlelight, sparkling tableware, and fresh flowers. Left, mix and match your favorite pieces to create a unique tablescape. Orange and red roses add a burst of color to a verdant table setting.

This cozy dining area was created from a niche located conveniently between the kitchen and the living room. Although it's more of a cubbyhole than an actual room, it has everything you need for the perfect setup.

An ordinary restaurant table (covered with a white tablecloth to disguise an unattractive top) is placed against the rustic red brick wall as if in an Italian trattoria. Two matching benches, each big enough for two, sit on either side. When you need additional seating, the table can be pulled away from the wall and extra chairs set at each end. Placing an old mantel mirror (unearthed at a junk store) two-thirds of the way down the wall gives diners a view of the rest of the room and adds depth to the tiny space. It also looks great with candlelight reflected in it. A single overhead lamp casts a warm glow over the table.

Of course, there's more to a dining room than just the table and chairs. Your choice of dishes and how you set your table affects the mood of the meal. Here, the table is dressed with a do-it-yourself mix including pieces of gold-rimmed glass, green milk glass, white china, and various patterns of silver. Although they were not designed as a set, the combination looks great together. Remember, your dishes don't all have to be in the same pattern. Eclectic place settings have a charm all their own, especially if you are picking up pieces over time at tag sales and flea markets, where you may not find a complete set anyway. But for a more cohesive look, try combining just two or three patterns. For example, on this table the soup bowls are from one set, the dessert plates and chargers are each from another. You may also try choosing wine or water goblets in the same style, but each in a different color—or in the same color but each in a different style.

smart tip

If the dishes you crave are unaffordable all at once, pass on the whole set and buy just the dinner plates or bowls, which you can mix in with what you already own.

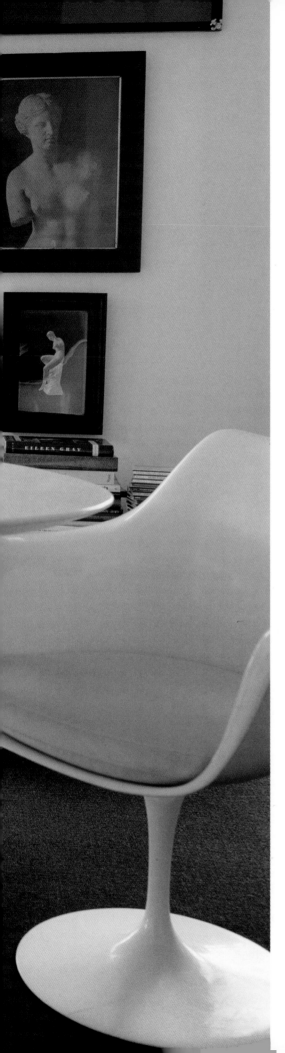

Fantastic plastic

In this light-filled dining room, traditional elements are combined with Eero Saarinen's thoroughly modern all-white Tulip table and chairs from the fifties. Since these dining sets were originally mass-produced, it's still possible to find them at vintage stores that specialize in furnishings from that decade. Or you may be fortunate enough to find them at a flea market or acquire them from a hip relative. But since collectors are finally beginning to appreciate these space-age designs, they can be quite costly, especially if they're in good condition. If you can't afford the real thing, you may want to look for imitations with similar lines, which might be less expensive.

When not used for dining, this table functions as a library table. Books are neatly stored on a nearby George Nelson bench, another fifties archetype. A neoclassical-style lamp, which can be adjusted for brightness, works for either entertaining or reading. The framed photographs on the wall feature Greek and Roman statuary, which fit the mood of this untraditional but still classic room.

By choosing white walls and monochromatic accessories from a different era, a mod dining room set stops short of kitsch. Instead it becomes a refreshing, modern space in which to entertain.

smart tip

In a room full of well-designed furniture with distinctive lines, keep accessories to a minimum. Clutter will only dilute the impact, especially if the pieces are simple.

tip

smart

When using an area in your kitchen for dining, don't forget the importance of ambient lighting. Since most kitchens come with ceiling fixtures, consider installing a dimmer switch, which is very easy to do. Or use indirect lighting, such as candles or a small lamp on the table.

Dining à deux

Set up on the far side of a long kitchen is a tiny dining area for two. Carefully composed vignettes, all of which are unified by the bold black-and-white checked floor underneath, create an informal dining atmosphere. Nineteenth-century spindle-back chairs are paired with a marble-and-iron bistro table. On top is a decorative arrangement, consisting of a rosemary topiary, new potatoes stacked in a porcelain compote, and a group of mangoes in an ironstone platter, each waiting its turn to be used in a delicious dish. Above, hung in a neat row, charcoal renderings of vessels are framed in wide white mattes and inexpensive black metal frames. On top of the radiator in front of the windowsill, a teal enamel pitcher holds a bunch of brilliant coral-colored roses. To the left, identical scalloped white plates, which are also used as serving platters, hang on the wall. Overhead, a simple rice-paper lampshade disguises and diffuses a bare bulb.

Along the opposite wall, industrial metro shelving holds all the components of a home office—a computer, fax, telephone, and files. When in use, either a chair is swung over to it or the work extends to the dining table. When the work is done, it's put neatly back in place.

Above, a dining room can be as simple as a table for two set up in the kitchen. A large pattern can work in a small space. Here, an oversized black-and-white checked floor energizes this tiny dining room, left. Don't overlook the beauty of everyday items. Fruits, vegetables, and herbs can be as lovely as flowers on the table.

the kitchen

Somewhere along the way, the kitchen became much more than a place to cook dinner. It now can be home to an office, the hub of a party, and the perfect place to hang out over coffee. But although you may be dreaming of a big kitchen where friends and family can gather, the reality is that most apartment kitchens are small. Some are so tiny there's barely room for a refrigerator and stove. But even if you're stuck with one of these galley kitchens, you can still—with a lot of ingenuity, but not a lot of money—create a stylish and very functional space.

If you know you're going to be living in your apartment for more than a few years, or if you own it, you may want to invest some money renovating or upgrading your kitchen. (A future buyer will appreciate—and often pay more for—a well-designed kitchen.) If that's your goal, don't overpersonalize the permanent features of the space. Not everyone will share your taste. Make your statement with paint, wallpaper, or funky decorations, which can be changed quickly, easily, and affordably.

If you're on a limited budget or have a short-term lease, choose your purchases carefully. In addition to paint and wallpaper, inexpensive touches such as new hardware and vintage dishes discovered at a flea market can transform a nondescript kitchen. Remember that clutter and kitsch can reduce space that may already be at a premium. As in the bathroom, if your kitchen is small, you will want to decorate with well-chosen pieces and colors instead of a lot of competing elements.

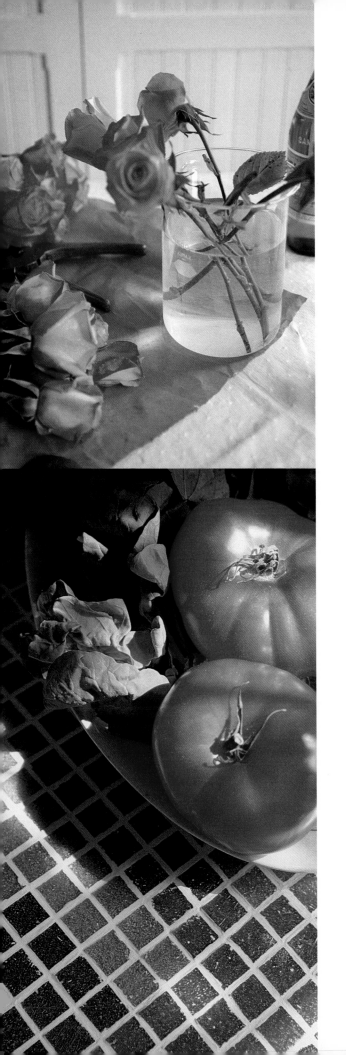

Country in the city

Even if you live in a city apartment, you don't have to give up your dream of a country kitchen. Since "country" can mean many different things to people, decide which elements appeal most to you (you certainly want to keep your modern-day appliances), and go from there.

In this kitchen, groundwork began underfoot. The floor was lightly sanded with a rented machine and finished with several coats of polyurethane for protection against spills and scuffs. Most farmhouse floors are left bare, so they can be swept clean with a broom or wiped with a mop—a convenience appreciated in the city, too.

Open shelving above the sink is not only a clever way to display a collection of bowls, stemware, soup tureens, plates, and pitchers, it also puts dishes within easy reach. Painting the surrounding wall, cabinet, and door a deep periwinkle blue makes the pieces seem to pop out. You won't overlook just the right one because it's hidden in the back of a dark cabinet.

A country kitchen wouldn't be complete without a big farmhouse table for friends and family to gather around. (It's also a great place to do paperwork, pay bills, or write letters.) It used to be quite easy to find inexpensive sturdy tables at flea markets or junk shops, but as they've become more and more desirable, prices have shot up. Don't despair; just keep your eyes open and check out off-the-beaten-path sources. This wooden table with beautifully carved legs and a rich veneer is an old school desk found on the street. It came with generations of initials carved on top and even a pencil drawer that can be used for storing flatware or napkins. Add chairs, old or new, and don't worry if they match or not.

A counter sided in traditional bead board was topped with an unexpected Mexican mosaic glass pattern in a sea of blues and greens. The tiny tiles are set into an aluminum frame custom-made for little money by a restaurant supply company (see page 167 for instructions). Since it's so labor-intensive, mosaic tile work is usually quite expensive. Here, the supplies are cheap and the labor—yours—free.

Previous page and above left, the big wooden table is used for working, arranging flowers, and, of course, dining. Left, a colorful countertop is created from precut glass tiles set into cement. Right, open shelving above the sink displays an assemblage of vintage dishes, glassware, and kitchen collectibles. A pantry is hidden inside the glossy white painted armoire.

French bistro

Oftentimes, the year in which your apartment building was built will dictate the style of your kitchen. And if you've got great period details—glass-front cabinets, French doors, and a black-and-white tile floor—why fight it? Half your work is already done. But just because your kitchen already has a certain style doesn't mean that you can't buy something from another era. Remember, in the past people didn't have access to the variety of materials and fixtures we have today. By blending different periods, you make a place uniquely your own.

Although this kitchen is in a 1920s American apartment building, it takes its cue from a classic French look. The two styles work well together because they're from the same era. Most of the furnishings in the kitchen are original, but a few affordable additions complete the look. The wall and hanging glass light fixtures (which may have once hung in a restaurant) were found at an architectural salvage shop. The sink faucet and nickel-plated drawer pulls and latches, however, were bought new at a renovator's supply store. If little work is needed in your kitchen, splurge on a few accessories.

Vintage tables such as this enamel-topped one still are easy to find since they were built to last. The 1930s office chairs were pretty beaten up when they were found in a junk store, but with a new coat of glossy white paint, they fit in perfectly with the rest of the decor.

Opposite, a kitchen table fits neatly into the breakfast nook. Above the table is a black-and-white print of a Paris bistro, shot during the thirties by Brassaï, known for his photographs that explored the city's seamier side of life. Above, glass French doors open onto a kitchen evocative of a Paris bistro.

smart tip

When looking for vintage fixtures, buy only pairs of faucets or sink handles. The chances of finding a "hot" for your "cold" are slim.

A great galley

Sometimes you just have to make the best out of a tight situation. This pint-sized kitchen, seen here through a bull's-eye mirror, is a study in efficiency. The tall cabinets were already part of the kitchen, but painted the same white as the tiled walls, they seem less obtrusive. The tops are used to store and display vases and cachepots—also in white— that are used infrequently.

Most of the walls in this kitchen are taken up by nonmovable storage, appliances, and fixtures. With only enough room for one decorative detail, it has to be special. The winner? An antique candle sconce and bull's-eye mirror that perfectly fills the narrow space between window and cabinet. And if everyday pieces such as canisters, pots and pans, and bottles are going to be kept out in the open, choose ones that are beautifully designed, even if it means spending a bit more money. Think of them as accessories, not just cooking utensils.

When renovating a small kitchen, opt for a small sink. As a bonus, you'll get more counter space.

Above, even with a small kitchen, you can still entertain large groups, but you may want to consider supplementing a fabulous homemade entrée with interesting take-out foods. Store drinks in the refrigerator and let guests help themselves. Right, a simple, well-designed clothes hamper takes the place of a traditional trash can.

Kitchen canvas

Art and creativity can flourish in a cookie-cutter contemporary apartment. And this can be accomplished with very little skill, money, or time. On the back wall of this standard black-and-white kitchen is a clever bulletin board made from canvas tacked over a thin sheet of cork. A black border was painted by hand around the edges. Invitations, magazine clippings, photos, take-out menus, and frequently used recipes can be changed as often as you choose—without leaving behind an army of holes. A touch of color is achieved with fresh fruit and flowers.

lighting

For a room to function properly, it needs proper lighting. But lighting is also an aesthetic choice, which sets the mood for a room. The right illumination can enhance a dreary space or make a small room seem larger. Before setting up additional lighting, consider the natural and artificial sources already there, looking at the room in both the daytime and the nightime. Then decide whether you need direct or indirect lighting, or a combination of both. ■ Direct lighting is best for when you need to concentrate on a task. If you have an eat-in kitchen, try an overhead fixture that can be dimmed for dining after you've prepared a meal. A halogen desk lamp provides a bright spot of light in a home office. An incandescent lamp with a 60-watt bulb is perfect for a bedside nightstand. ■ Indirect lighting contributes to the ambience of a room. Set candles throughout the room for a romantic mood. Or you may want to install sconces—small light fixtures that project out from the wall—which provide a soft glow. Or torchères, which project light upward to reflect off the ceiling. A halogen floor lamp will provide bright light for a fairly large amount of space. ■ The fixtures or lamps themselves should also be considered carefully. A beautiful table lamp may be a decorative note, or you may want fixtures that blend unobtrusively into the surroundings.

Cottage charm

You can give a modern kitchen a cozy cottage feel without a major renovation. Begin by working with whatever kind of cabinetry and appliances already exist and concentrate on what you can change quickly and cheaply. For instance, consider using fabric for something other than curtains or seat cushions; fabric can add color and texture to walls, too. Here, a blue-and-white linen fabric with an old-fashioned country scene (known as toile de Jouy) was applied directly to walls—an easy technique that uses only starch and water (see instructions on page 182). Instead of framed art, two large ceramic platters are hung on the wall. Bright red Gerbers are placed in an everyday glass decanter and a blue ceramic bowl holds Granny Smith apples.

Remember, paint isn't only for walls. Opposite, a few coats of color on dark cabinets dramatically transform a formerly dingy kitchen. Left, use fabric the same way you would wallpaper to impart a warm, cozy feel to kitchen walls.

A new look

Now a cheerful and lively room, this kitchen started out as dark and uninviting because of ugly brown wooden cabinets. Replacing or refinishing them was too costly. Instead, an inexpensive can of paint was employed to give them a fresh new look. Since the rest of the room, including walls and floors, is white, any color would fit in. However, this shade of milk-glass green goes with the collection of enamel cookware from the 1950s that is used frequently. Affordable accessories such as dish towels and teacups continue to carry the new color theme through. Overhead, casting a bright glow, is a Deco light fixture, which replaced an old nondescript one. A vintage soda fountain stool, covered in pink vinyl, provides a comfortable seat while peeling potatoes or drinking cappuccino.

smart tip

It's easy and inexpensive to replace a light fixture, but remember to hold on to the old one so you can replace it when you leave and take yours with you.

The kitchen heats up

A kitchen that opens onto your living room can be wonderful for the cook who doesn't want to be shut away when preparing meals. But sometimes you need privacy or, at the very least, a way of hiding kitchen clutter from guests. One way to accomplish this is with sliding rice-paper screens, inspired by Japanese shoji screens, which can easily be closed. Even when they're open, they subtly separate rooms without seeming intrusive.

The rest of this plain white kitchen is dressed up with bowls, pitchers, and utensils that provide a much-needed burst of color. Wooden bar stools are painted bright red and an old enamel dental cabinet, now functioning as a mini-bar, is painted green.

smart tip

Screens are inexpensive to buy already assembled, or you can make your own by stapling or gluing paper or fabric onto an unfinished wood screen. Black is the most traditional color, but paint the frame any color you like, or leave it as is.

Right, think up new uses for favorite old pieces. Here, an old dental cabinet was painted with enamel paint and now houses a mini-bar. Terra-cotta planters hold fruit and a hanging Shaker basket on the wall stores spare candles. Top, bright red stools and colorful kitchenware keep an all-white kitchen from looking too sterile. Above, a variety of clear glass jars hold staples—beans, pasta, and grains.

Fifties update

To update a 1950s kitchen quickly and easily, begin by painting kitchen cabinets with a fresh coat of white enamel and replacing old-style knobs with slick, new silver ones. (Knobs should unscrew easily.) Then add a thoroughly modern backsplash of porcelain tiles cut into rectangles. If you're willing to mix up colors and shapes, you can buy close-outs, samples, and remainders of tile quite cheaply. In fact, some tile stores give them away. You will probably need a few of them cut to fit, which you can do yourself inexpensively with a rented tile cutter, or have it done at the store; they will probably cut them for free or a nominal charge. Measure the space and figure out how many tiles will fit, and how much space will be left over. Make sure you calculate the 1/8-inch grout space between tiles into your measurment.

A stainless-steel restaurant rolling table provides extra storage and countertop space as an island or against a wall. You can purchase one at a restaurant supply store or even custom-order one to size. Since it's made for professionals, it's sturdy enough to survive countless moves. Alongside, a curvy iron bar stool provides a comfortable seat.

Right, an aluminum candelabrum adds a whimsical touch to the kitchen. Even practical items can be beautiful. Above, an herb garden is planted in a terra-cotta pot that is painted, then distressed with sandpaper. Dishwashing detergent is housed in an empty olive oil bottle with an added spout—much prettier than the original plastic squeeze container.

smart tip

Keep favorite cookbooks where you need them: in the kitchen. Set aside a shelf or part of cabinet to hold your collection, but be sure to keep them away from sources of heat, steam, and grease.

the bedroom

Even when you were a kid, your bedroom was your haven. Whether you simply covered the walls with posters or came up with ingenious ways to personalize the space you shared with a sibling, it was here that you made your first stab at designing a room. But now you need clever solutions for damaged walls, poor closet space, scuffed floors, and insufficient light—a few posters of your favorite rock stars just won't cut it.

Every bedroom requires a few essentials, such as a comfortable bed and a few great pillows. You'll also want a bedside table for an alarm clock, your current favorite books, a good reading light, maybe a telephone, and a notepad. If there's space in the room, add an overstuffed chair or chaise.

But it's the personal touches—childhood toys, souvenirs from trips, goofy photos that you're not quite ready to share with just anyone—that make it feel like your sanctuary.

Lately, though, the bedroom has evolved into much more than a place to sleep. For convenience sake, or because of space demands, it's become the room of choice for a home office, TV, or sewing room, extra storage, or a workout area.

Bright ideas

The theme of this bedroom reflects a love of color and a passion for objects from around the world as seen in wall hangings, paintings, masks, trimmings, and accessories. But the exotic paint job has a more pragmatic side: It cleverly disguises damaged walls in need of repair. An intricate pattern, inspired by the Tibetan fabric panel that hangs over the window, provides a fast solution to surface flaws. It was accomplished by first sponging and stenciling the walls with regular latex wall paint. Although this technique can take several days to accomplish, it's quicker and cheaper than replastering walls.

A window without a view is covered with a panel of Tibetan fabric. The French doors (which lead to a small terrace) were stripped of generations of paint and left in their original state. Straw Mexican Christmas ornaments and nineteenth-century tiebacks hold back the heavy velvet striped drapes—a funky combination.

Remember that just because something is an antique doesn't necessarily mean it's expensive. And buying the original version can even be cheaper or the same price as a new one—and it's usually better constructed. This is especially true with furniture and hardware. Old doorknobs, hinges, drawer pulls, curtain rods, tiebacks, and switch plates—often made of brass or nickel-plated —can be found at flea markets, antiques shops, even hardware stores that have been in business for generations (you may have to ask to see them if they're not on display).

Throughout this bedroom, books are casually piled on the floor and on top of tables. This may serve as a solution if you're a booklover faced with limited or no shelf space. Books are very fragile and easily damaged by excess weight or water rings. Placing objects or plants on them should be done with the utmost care.

Previous page, a stenciled wall border and firm pillows take the place of a traditional headboard. Top, a circus of color can still be soothing in a bedroom, depending on the shades and combinations. Try choosing earth tones such as ocher, terra-cotta, and slate blue interspersed with spots of brighter shades. Above, an artful arrangement of objects. Left, a corner of the bedroom provides space for a desk.

First-class sleeper

Although sleep is a number one priority in any bedroom, ample storage is often a close second. Even the most generous closets never seem to be enough. Here, stacked leather suitcases (found at a junk store) serve as a bedside stand and store out-of-season bedding and clothes. On top is a cozy arrangement of books, family photos, a mugful of glasses and pens, and a tole vase for fresh flowers. An old lampshade gets an instant update by wrapping it in a sheer leopard-print scarf. To top it off, a famous Irving Penn photo, originally published in *Vogue* in 1950, sits pretty.

Borrow some ideas from the living room to give your bedroom a fashionable new look. Duvets and shams (essentially slipcovers for comforters and pillows) instantly transform a room. They come ready-made or you can stitch up your own from fabric or flat sheets. Here, dressmaker details make all the difference, as pillows are covered in cream fabric with brown-covered buttons, while the comforter is done in the reverse—brown fabric with cream-covered buttons.

Flea market finds and old keepsakes create a personal still life on top of a nightstand made of stacked vintage luggage, which doubles as storage.

smart tip

You may be tempted to cover your bed with dozens of decorative pillows in all sorts of shapes and colors. But be prepared that every night you'll have to find a place to store them (or throw them on the floor), only to rearrange them again in the morning.

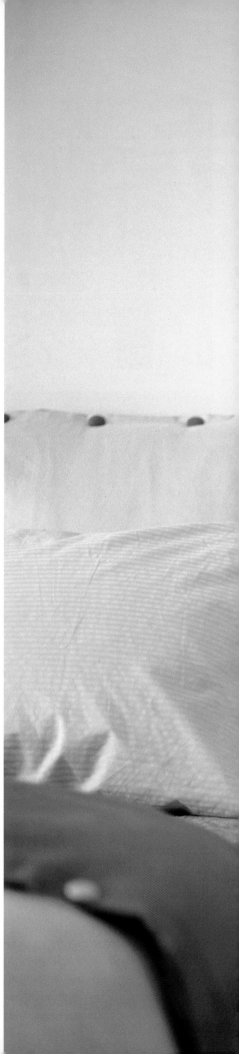

Royal flush

Inspiration for a room can come from an endless variety of sources, such as historical houses, literature, even a period film. The regal look of this bedroom was derived from the popular movie *The Madness of King George,* in which bright white and bold red dominated in the sets and costumes. The white iron bed, which looks even brighter contrasted against royal purple walls, is dressed to perfection in crisp white sheets and a rich red-and-white velvet-and-damask striped duvet. The bed skirt was fashioned from a red-and-white gingham fabric.

Curtain panels were sewn from linen fabric bought by the yard and hemmed on the top and bottom. Using black metal curtains rings that easily clasp onto the edge of the fabric, they hang from an iron curtain rod. Since linen is somewhat sheer, an opaque Roman shade, made from the same striped fabric used for the duvet, hangs behind the curtains to block out light at night.

The cabinet next to the bed is actually an old school locker, rescued from the street and given a fresh coat of red paint. The locker's enamel 189 plaque was found at a Paris flea market. Mix your flea market finds together to create something entirely new. Sitting on top, rotary dial phones, found at flea markets in both the United States and Paris, are considered highly collectible in this age of Touch-Tone technology.

The crowning touch in this room is the Greek keystone-and-laurel-wreath border hand-painted using a transfer technique (see page 164 for instructions). First, the red border is applied with a brush and the pattern is traced over it, using graphite tracing paper. Then the key pattern is filled in with two coats of white paint. Metallic gold paint is used for the laurel wreaths.

Left, three well-chosen colors—red, purple, and white—were used in this room to create the feel of a royal bedchamber. A rose marble-topped iron stand circa 1925 is an untraditional night table. Above right, hanging by a red velvet ribbon is a vintage postcard celebrating the birthday of George Washington. Check your family attic, flea markets, and garage sales for beautifully illustrated old postcards, which can often be bought for less than a dollar. Right, a sheer linen curtain allows light in while a striped Roman shade blocks it out.

White nights

Here, white is used in a tiny bedroom to maximize space and light while creating a peaceful and comfortable environment. Nothing is more cooling on a warm summer night or more soothing after a hard day at the office than pure white bed linens.

To begin, the room was drenched in a rich creamy shade. Windows are covered with inexpensive rice paper and bamboo shades (available at home department stores and Asian home furnishing stores), which allow plenty of light to stream in but provide privacy from nearby neighbors. Sunlight reflects off mirrors hung behind and next to the bed. And for nighttime reading, lamps are strategically hung from the wall on both sides of the bed. Additional illumination comes from an old ceramic lamp that sits like a Buddha on a folding bamboo chair.

Left, this room appears larger than it actually is thanks to mirrors and a lavish use of white. Above, white can be carried through to your art and accessories.

pillows

Functional as well as decorative, throw pillows are an affordable design accessory. They can change the look of an old sofa or enliven a plain-Jane chair. And if you can't afford new furnishings, you can always buy or make a pillow or two to give a room new life. ■ If you decide to construct your own pillow cover, you may choose to indulge in more expensive fabrics since you only need a few feet of material. Or seek out vintage patterns at flea markets (just make sure that they're not torn or frayed if the pillows will be used frequently). If you want a more coordinated look, fashion your pillows out of the same fabric as something else in the room, such as your curtains, or you might choose a fabric that has the same pattern as another upholstered furnishing in the room, but in different colors. ■ Be creative with finishing touches: mix solid colors to form a checkerboard, striped, or harlequin pattern; add a ruffle along the edge; employ contrasting buttons instead of a zipper; use raffia as a tie closure. These same tips can be used to dress up store-bought pillows, too. Pillows can be a minimal investment that allow you to inexpensively add character to your apartment.

The metal urge

The need for a home office determined the layout and design of this sleek bedroom. And its clean, uncluttered lines make it comfortable to both work and sleep in. But a word of caution before moving your desk into your bedroom: Make sure you keep your work space as separate as possible from your sleeping space—it's hard to get a good night's sleep when the last thing you see is a pile of unfinished paperwork.

Here, furnishings in a variety of metals were designed to complement each other. When the right-sized desk could not be found, a custom-made stainless-steel table (made by a restaurant supplier) was created to fit neatly under the window and above the radiator. It's just wide enough to hold a computer and a minimum of desk accessories—pen and pencil holders, note-pad, and a small but powerful halogen desk lamp —to cut down on clutter. For an original look, the iron gallery shelf on the wall was also commissioned for the room. Commissioning a piece can sometimes be a money saver in the long run, especially if you end up buying a ready-made piece that doesn't suit your needs in the future. Take some time to think about long-term needs before you have something made. Check out unusual sources such as welders, restaurant suppliers, and cabinetmakers in addition to furniture designers.

Above, the desk is sited in front of the bedroom's oversized window to take advantage of the natural light for working. Narrow venetian blinds can be tightly rolled up to reveal as much window as possible during the day, but when dropped down at night, they effectively block out light. Opposite, above, an iron sleigh bed is flanked by a Biedermeier table —completely covered with framed photos. While Biedermeier's heavy simplicity was considered inferior bourgeois furniture in Germany when it was introduced in the nineteenth century, it is highly appreciated by collectors today. Opposite, left, a narrow metal shelf (inexpensively custommade for this space at a metal shop) holds a row of family photos, votive candles, and tiny glasses filled with single white tulips at the foot of the bed.

smart tip

If space is at a premium, think about using a stool, which can tuck under a desk or table and take up less space than a chair.

Nature's palette

The pale sky blue walls and soft sage green–painted furniture combined with cool snow-white fabrics create a soothing, inviting environment in which to relax in this bedroom. A long panel of linen fabric was draped like a canopy over the bed's iron posts to soften the hard edges (you can also try old tablecloths, gauze, striped cotton sheets, or Indian saris). Tiny crystal drops in the shape of leaves (found in a notions shop) were sewn along the edges to reflect the light.

A Victorian chair bought at a junk shop was professionally recovered in a blue velvet to complement the walls. An old linen cupboard is a clever piece of storage: It now hides the TV and VCR, as well as magazines. (Don't use a fine antique for a television cabinet since you'll need to drill holes in the back to accommodate wiring.)

Opposite, a sun-shaped mirror hangs over the entrance to the bedroom, inside of which the white-covered bed takes center stage. The round table beside it acts as a nightstand and dressing table (a small black stool slides underneath when not being used). Above left, a linen cupboard serves as an entertainment center while also storing magazines, videos, and books. Left, a pen-and-ink drawing hangs like a window on the cabinet. Overleaf, left, a small seating area is made complete by a comfortable reading chair and a desk that does double duty as a nightstand. Overleaf, right, a glass tumbler filled with blue hyacinth sits amid beautifully displayed objects.

A thousand and one nights

Lush patterns and decorative fabrics create a sense of richness and splendor—without a lot of money. Don't be afraid to mix interesting colors and patterns. Entering this bedroom is like stepping into the pages of *A Thousand and One Arabian Nights.* You feel as if you were let loose in a sumptuous foreign bazaar. Rich paisley patterns and warm spice colors transform this bedroom into an exotic Middle Eastern boudoir. A trompe l'oeil mural in the hallway (seen through the open door) leads you to this room like a path, and prepares you for what lies ahead.

The bedroom's padded fabric walls not only give the room a cozy tentlike feel, they also help absorb outside noise from nearby neighbors and the street. This can be done by first stapling batting to the wall and then stapling fabric over it. To finish along the edges you can hot-glue braided trim or welting. Another way to apply fabric to your walls is with starch (see instructions on page 182).

Opposite, a mini-canopy is created above the bed from Mexican blankets lined with red. Right, beautiful lamp shades are not only expensive, they can be hard to find. An alternative: Hand-paint a cheap lamp shade. The gold stars and stripes on this one match the exotic decor in the rest of the bedroom. Above right, a skirted writing table covered in the same fabric as the walls provides extra storage space underneath.

A liberated look

You don't have to sacrifice style in a space that you'll only be living in for a short time. Just be careful to put your money into what you will be taking with you—furniture and accessories—when you move.

In a bedroom without much architectural interest, instant drama is introduced with a few strokes of color and pattern. Set against plain white walls, the bed is covered in a wool plaid blanket that immediately makes the room look warm and welcoming. Above the bed is a striking painted canvas of the Statue of Liberty, which substitutes for a headboard and is reflected in the mirrored closet doors. If need be, the painting can be easily removed from its frame and rolled up when you leave. Any kind of fabric, decorated or not, can be hung in this fashion.

On either side of the bed are inexpensive metal folding tables, which you can always find use for in your next place if you don't need them for nightstands. They can be set up in the living room or even in an outdoor space. A saturated chartreuse quilted chair commands the corner. Be sure to make room for what's important to you in your bedroom, but also know when it's time to compromise.

Above, a wall of mirrored closets reflects the bed and the vividly painted canvas above it, making the room seem larger than it actually is. Opposite, the bedroom door was painted chartreuse for an unexpected addition of color.

smart tip

Don't rely on small-scale furnishings to make a tiny bedroom seem bigger. Large-scale pieces, such as this painting used as a headboard, can give a room impact.

Wake-up call

Sometimes all it takes is one targeted stroke of decorating brilliance to provide punch to a bedroom. In this tiny space (barely bigger than a double bed), it's accomplished with a brightly colored window treatment. A tomato red zigzag valance (cut from fabric and attached to the window frame with Velcro) hangs over curtains created from a playful selection of colorful fabrics.

You don't always have to camouflage a small space with pale colors (and you may not even want to). Instead, go for the dazzling shades you love. Go ahead and buy a pistachio-colored comforter. Paint the bed-side table green. Even the flowers beside the bed are chosen for their color—bright red and orange poppies. Then hang one big piece of art instead of a lot of small ones. In this room, the painting of an oversized teapot seems ready to burst from its frame, which goes along with the whimsical personality of the room. The fact of the matter is that a tiny room isn't always going to look a whole lot bigger just because it's painted white.

Stripe it rich

Sometimes a strong dose of color is all a lackluster space needs to give it energy. And nothing adds punch more intensely than red. A shot of white from the double set of pillows makes the reds look even stronger.

A variety of reds are used throughout the bedroom to create a sensuous setting that seems slightly enigmatic. On the walls are hand-painted crimson stripes, which also help hide damaged plaster (see page 169 for instructions). Combining two shades of the same color in the room provides texture while keeping it from looking too saturated. Deep bordeaux velvet drapes are hung from an iron rod.

And accessories are used to enhance the mystery. A Chinese lantern sways gently over the nightstand. An exotic Casablanca lily is placed in a bright yellow McCoy vase. A beveled mahogany mirror rests provocatively against the wall.

Above, bright colors play a big role in a small bedroom. Left, lace-trimmed pillows add a touch of innocence to a sensuous red room.

smart tip

When storage space is limited, put unused space— such as that underneath your bed—to good use. Use boxes or bins, preferably with lids to keep out dust, and attach wheels to make them easy to slide in and out.

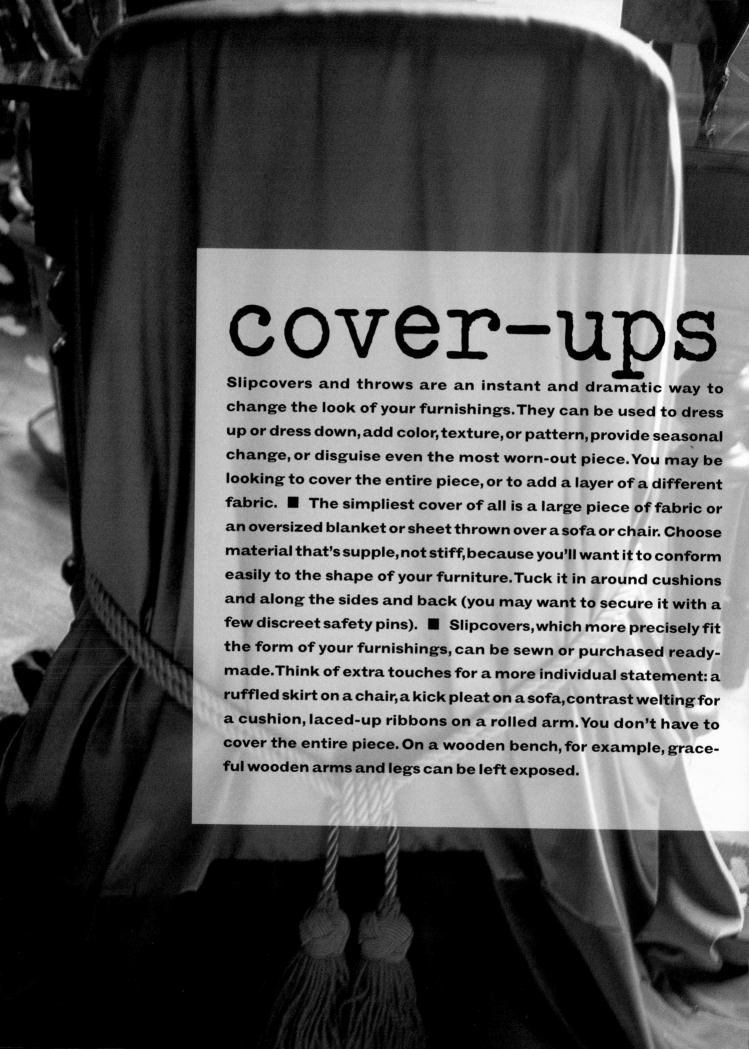

cover-ups

Slipcovers and throws are an instant and dramatic way to change the look of your furnishings. They can be used to dress up or dress down, add color, texture, or pattern, provide seasonal change, or disguise even the most worn-out piece. You may be looking to cover the entire piece, or to add a layer of a different fabric. ■ The simpliest cover of all is a large piece of fabric or an oversized blanket or sheet thrown over a sofa or chair. Choose material that's supple, not stiff, because you'll want it to conform easily to the shape of your furniture. Tuck it in around cushions and along the sides and back (you may want to secure it with a few discreet safety pins). ■ Slipcovers, which more precisely fit the form of your furnishings, can be sewn or purchased ready-made. Think of extra touches for a more individual statement: a ruffled skirt on a chair, a kick pleat on a sofa, contrast welting for a cushion, laced-up ribbons on a rolled arm. You don't have to cover the entire piece. On a wooden bench, for example, graceful wooden arms and legs can be left exposed.

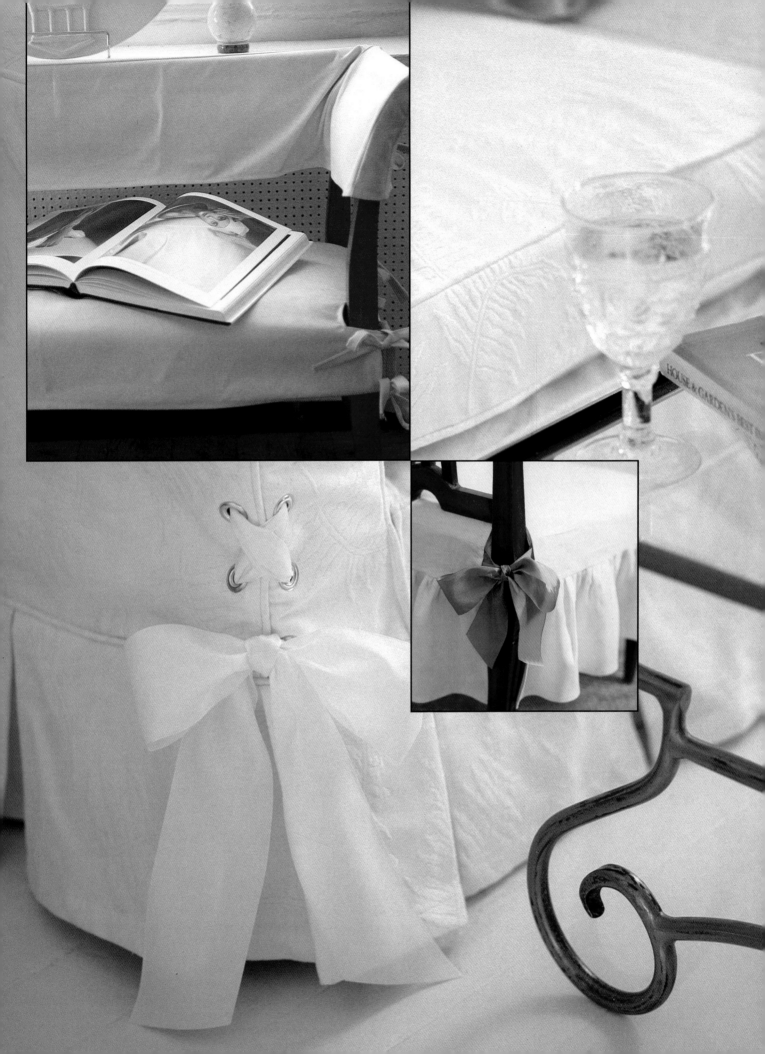

A wealth of material

You don't have to rely on white and lace if you want to create a soft, romantic look in your bedroom. Instead, mix muted colors and blend soft patterns together. Here, everything from stripes to florals is layered on the bed. Although there's seemingly a lot going on, the neutral palette helps to create a peaceful environment.

To keep the focus on the bed, walls are painted a soothing vanilla. The drapes are simply a pair of inexpensive twin sheets (use a blend of 50 percent cotton, 50 percent polyester for easy, no-iron care) attached with clip-on rings to an iron curtain rod. The pale color of the sheets allows for plenty of light to flood through. If you want less light or to obscure an unpleasant view, pick a darker sheet. Busy patterns draw attention to windows, while using the same color sheets as on the bed creates a coordinated look.

An unfinished bedside stand is painted a sunny yellow with a white top and pulls for contrast. The gold swirl stamps on top make it more special. If you can't find ready-made rubber stamps that you like, create your own from an eraser or potato (see instructions on page 181).

To make a window seem larger, hang your curtain rod a few inches above the frame and extend the brackets on either side.

smart tip

Right, although this room is filled with an array of patterns —even the wooden headboard has a vivid grain—the room stays tranquil thanks to a soft color palette. Above, swirls, similar to the curves of the wire flower basket, are stamped on top of the bedside table with a rubber stamp and metallic paint.

Forties hollywood

By employing a few simple tricks with fabric and color and paying attention to period details, you can achieve high style on a small budget. Stepping into this retro bedroom is like taking a trip back in time to the alluring Hollywood glamour of the 1940s.

First, walls are covered in a scattered red berry-print wallpaper, which is also a great cover-up if walls are less than perfect. The large-scale floral print on pillow shams and the duvet cover is the companion pattern to the wallpaper. Pairing these traditional prints with a contrasting crimson-and-white fabric gives the room a fresh feel. The scooped padded headboard is a weekend project that you can make with cheap plywood, muslin batting, and fabric in the pattern of your choice (see instructions on page 184).

Well-chosen details such as the carved alabaster lamp and rotary telephone on the bedside table complete the retro look of this room.

smart tip

To determine how much wallpaper you'll need in a room, measure the height of the room from floor to ceiling and multiply by the width of all four walls added together. Divide this number by the square feet per roll of your pattern. Be sure to calculate for windows and doors, and buy some extra paper in case of mistakes.

the bathroom

Take your bath as seriously as you would any other room in your apartment: Define the space and give it style. Comfort is very important, so indulge in big, fluffy towels, rich soaps, and great-looking fixtures. Your bathroom should also be a space that's easy to clean, which means keeping decorations to a minimum. Make sure you have enough convenient surface space for the basic essentials, and sufficient storage—whether a free-standing piece, a built-in cabinet, or a hanging shelf—to house other toiletries.

Your bathroom should be be a place in which you can both unwind and get reinvigorated. Make sure the lighting is bright but not harsh, and keep candles on hand: Their warm glow can help you relax during a luxurious bath. Although you may be limited by the size of your bathroom, you shouldn't be limited by humdrum ideas.

A natural retreat

When you own your apartment, it's worthwhile to invest some time and money in refurbishing your bathroom. When the fixtures and floor in this bathroom needed to be replaced, they were given the same care and attention to detail as would have been given any other room in the apartment.

Walls received special treatment with a striae paint job that demands time, but not money. To create the effect here, two different shades of pear green were used (see instructions on page 180). Above the sink is a mirror that was framed in birch plywood. The scroll pattern was painted on freehand with regular black latex paint and sealed with a coat of polyurethane.

The porcelain-tiled checkerboard floor is laid out on a 45 degree angle, which makes the space seem grander. The eight-point stars were custom-cut at the tile company—which costs a little extra, but the look is fabulous. Or buy cheap tile in fun colors and lay it down at a 45 degree angle to create this same spacious illusion. Black is used as an accent color to lend a graphic quality to the room.

Above, a small wire and wicker bench takes up very little room, yet provides a much-needed spot for extra towels. Previous page, choosing a sink with built-in racks is also a smart way to sneak in extra storage. Opposite, a vintage chenille bedspread makes a wonderful, inexpensive shower curtain (and can be tossed in the washing machine). Whites, greens, pinks, and blues are easy to find at flea markets or garage sales; choose a color that works well in your bathroom.

Bathing beauty

When you're faced with an ordinary white tile bath, accessorize it the same way you would a simple little dress. Everything you add should enhance the lines, not turn it into a fashion victim. To smarten up this tiny bath, walls are dressed in a crisp green-and-white striped wallpaper that accentuates the single green floral tile set among the white ones. Place a silver filigreed box on top of a plain porcelain dish to hold your soap in style. Instead of a regular glass, choose a special one, like this opaque glass decorated with attractive gold swirls, found at a garage sale. Opt for a toothbrush in a pretty frosted shade—it's the small details that make a difference.

The shower curtain is made out of a vintage chenille coverlet by punching holes along the top (see instructions, page 170). Other materials to consider: terry cloth, cotton piqué, seersucker, or ordinary bedsheets. Just make sure to hang a plastic liner behind the material to avoid damaging delicate fabric or getting water on your floor, and don't use any fabric that is very valuable, because water and steam will take their toll over time.

Ocean side

Combine the beautiful lines of antiquity with the clean, simple look of twentieth-century modernism in your bath. Choose a classical motif such as these giant waves that are appliquéd onto a linen shower curtain (see page 170 for instructions), and then carry that theme through with your accessories. On the plain glass shelf above the sink sits family treasures that have been put to use: a blue porcelain box decorated with an acanthus-leaf scroll, along with a silverplated goblet, bud vase, and dish, which has a delicate beaded edge.

If your apartment comes with an original pedestal or porcelain sink, don't ruin its simple lines by adding a vanity. Instead, look for storage ideas elsewhere, such as the glass shelf under the mirror. Place a small bench, cabinet, or magazine rack in a corner to hold extra towels. If no space is to be found in the bathroom, set aside a shelf in a nearby closet for toiletries.

Right, look beyond obvious racks and shelves for storage solutions. A mahogany pedestal can hold extra towels, while a mulberry transferware bowl can be filled with soap. Above, keep everyday necessities within easy reach, but toss away unsightly packaging. On the glass shelf above the sink is a silverplated cup full of cotton swabs. A blue porcelain box hides cotton balls.

A standard-sized shower curtain can look short in a bathroom with high ceilings. Add length by sewing a wide border of fabric to the bottom for your own custom curtain.

smart tip

Sleight of hand

It's easy to transform a simple bath into an elegant spa-like retreat, thanks to a few clever tricks. A good way to begin is by choosing a neutral color palette. Here, floor-to-ceiling furnishings (including the towels and bath mat) are all in a soft sandy shade.

But it's the extra touches that make this bath so glamorous. Gold, silver, and copper leaf (available at art supply stores) have been brushed onto the ceiling molding to make the room glow. You can also apply the same treatment in smaller doses to your tissue-box holder or wastepaper basket; don't overdo it—you can move from elegant to gaudy if you use a heavy hand. Tasseled fringe was attached to the top of the shower curtain. Instead of framing the fish prints individually and ending up with a dozen small pictures, they were framed as a group, making one enormous picture with a big impact.

To make the most out of limited storage space, purchase the longest towel bar you can find, or have one cut to fit from an ordinary plumbing pipe or a curtain rod. Installing it the length of your wall increases your storage space and gives you more flexibility.

Don't hang valuable art or original photographs in the bathroom, since heat and moisture can ruin them. Instead, frame postcards, museum reproductions, or illustrations from magazines.

smart tip

Take the plunge

Although you shouldn't shy away from using large patterns in a bath, it helps to have a good source of light and a high ceiling to keep things in balance—especially if your room is small. In this bath, walls are covered in an Oriental toile-patterned paper. A three-inch-wide grosgrain ribbon, which mimics the black tile border along the wall, finishes off the shower curtain. You can attach the ribbon by sewing or fusing it to the fabric. Kept closed, an opaque shower curtain also hides uneven or damaged ceramic tiles.

Left, your eye can't help but be drawn to the red-framed print, bold against the black-and-white background. Opposite, a combination of beautiful materials—tile, marble, gold leaf, and sheer crepe fabric—gives this small bathroom a luxurious look.

storage

No matter how big your apartment is or how many closets you have, it always seems that you never have enough storage space. But the key to stylish and orderly living is to organize your things so that they're integrated into the overall design of your apartment. ■ A good way to begin is by grouping things together. If you don't have enough shelf space, books can be stacked on top of a bench, table, or even the floor. And this way they're all in one place when you need to locate the one you need. Buy unusual but inexpensive tin containers, terra-cotta flowerpots, or flea market pottery to hold bunches of pens and pencils on your desk. In the kitchen, toss away unattractive packaging and store dry goods such as grains and beans in clear glass containers. ■ Discover the hidden storage spaces in your apartment. Hide luggage or out-of-season clothing under your bed. An old trunk can provide a table surface while holding extra linens or anything that's not frequently needed. Use decorative wicker baskets or wooden boxes to hide your filing, CDs, video and audio cassettes. Wire bins, filing cabinets, or cardboard boxes can be tucked under a table and covered with a pretty tablecloth. ■ Use ordinary things in new and different ways. A small wire shelf found at a flea market can hold toiletries in the bathroom. Hang a collection of bracelets and necklaces on a coatrack next to the sink. An armoire in the bedroom hides the TV as well as a collection of magazines and pottery.

Bathing suite

Think you can't squeeze another inch of storage from your bath? Here, a wire-frame basket and shelf scavenged from the curbside are used to hold extra linens and bath supplies that aren't used every day; the open weave allows air to flow through to keep things dry. An inexpensive basket that loops over the showerhead (available in any housewares store) neatly holds shampoos, conditioners, and soaps that normally clutter the rim of the tub. A starfish anchors a washcloth on the edge of the sink.

Make use of the wasted space high up on your shower wall by hanging shelves to hold items that won't be affected by moisture. Opposite, apothecary jars and a seashell box neatly store toiletries.

one-room living

Living in a one-room space can mean anything from an enormous downtown city loft to a tiny studio apartment in a converted Victorian house. All such spaces share a few common traits. For instance, unlike a conventional apartment where each room was intended for a particular purpose—"kitchen," "bedroom," "living room"—a one-room space is open to just about any kind of configuration.

Before you go about setting up your furniture, think about your needs. If you're living in a large open loft, you have a lot more room to play around with than in a studio apartment. Nonetheless, many of the same principles apply. You'll probably want to delineate some traditional areas: a place to sleep, eat, and lounge and watch television. But you may also want to set aside room for a home office or dining area. And you'll probably need to create some inventively stylish storage space since, more than likely, it will be out in the open. Try to keep the flow of the apartment as open as possible, both to make your place seem larger and to make the most of its wall-less environment.

MODERN FURNITURE CLASSICS
FRANCE
COLOR

Jewel box

If you love color, use it lavishly but wisely in a small space. Here, in an L-shaped studio, pastel walls serve as a sophisticated background for the vibrant colors used throughout. Two of the walls are painted a soft, cool green while the opposite two are covered in a pale shade of orchid.

The center of the apartment becomes a jewel-like setting due to saturated color. The sofa, in need of reupholstering but awaiting the funds, is temporarily covered with a blanket. A blanket is not only inexpensive, it allows you the flexibility to change the apartment's look according to the seasons or your mood. For a winter look, the sofa is covered with a warm chenille blanket in a carnelian red. Splurge on pillow fabrics such as this leopard-print and gold and magenta silk shantung, since you don't need more than half a yard. For summer, the sofa is covered with a white Marseilles coverlet with scalloped edges, and more silk shantung pillows.

The living area also doubles as an informal dining room where guests can pull up a chair, plop down on pillows, or sit on the soft rug. Glass goblets from the 1930s, collected at tag sales and flea markets, make beautiful votive centerpieces. Above the sofa is a set of orchid prints originally from a vintage botanical book. Attractive prints like these can be purchased at junk shops and flea markets for as little as 25 cents. If

You don't have to edit down your possessions simply because you're living in a studio apartment, but organization and clearly defined areas help make the space livable. A beat-up sofa becomes a focal point of the room when covered with a blanket, which changes seasonally. In winter (previous page), the sofa is topped with red chenille, while in summer (left) it's hidden beneath a white Marseilles coverlet.

you're framing something worth pre-
serving, remember you can purchase
acid-free paper and mattes for a
fraction more than regular ones.

The white iron bed, which provides
additional seating in a pinch, is
topped with a pale purple Marseilles
coverlet and a "Wedding Ring" patterned quilt. A word of caution:
Handmade quilts, new or antique, are
very fragile—and valuable. If you like
the look, but yours needs to withstand
a lot of wear or a beloved pet, you
may want to purchase a machine-
made one of lesser quality. Although
the detailing is not as fine, it will
stand up to everyday use—and you
won't be heartbroken if it's stained or
torn. On the bedside table is an
etched-glass lamp topped with a per-
sonalized shade that's easy to make,
this one with blue and white stripes
(see page 162 for instructions).

If you need to set up a home
office in an open-floor plan, concentrate on establishing good storage so
work doesn't overflow into your living space. Extra-wide metro shelving, cheaper in restaurant supply
stores than in most home shops,
keeps papers, books, and even a fax
machine neat in a decorative way.
Paper- or fabric-covered boxes hold
office supplies while painted wooden
crates hold files.

Above, a narrow space between two windows is the perfect
candidate for a home office. The only thing you wouldn't
normally find in a living room is the computer. Right, here, a
shelf in the sleeping area holds not only books but rarely
used serving pieces. Tucked inside are photos, bills, and
letters. Overleaf, right, pretty wicker baskets and pottery
are used to hold office supplies, and the lamp has a soft
parchment paper shade, not typical office supply items.
Overleaf, left, nothing about this wall screams "office."
Metal shelving, which stands out against the pale lavender
wall, shows off a decorative mix of books, files, and
ceramics. In a studio where storage is at a premium, you
may need to resort to some uncommon solutions.

smart tip

One gallon of paint will cover approximately
400 square feet of primed wall. Unprimed
walls take twice as much.

Close quarters

One of the most important considerations in a studio apartment is where to put your sleeping area. Although a sofa bed is an obvious solution, you have to open it up every night and close it in the morning. And it's not very relaxing to sleep in the same spot where you watch TV, entertain friends, and maybe even eat dinner. Yet you don't want to have a bed floating in the middle of your apartment. A happy solution is to create two distinct areas and separate them with a screen. A screen effectively shields your bed from the rest of the room, but allows air and light to circulate. The one here is padded with Eco-fil batting, made of Fortrel EcoSpun recycled fibers, and covered in a reversible velvet fabric (see instructions on page 186).

To make the bedroom area a little more intimate than the more public area, cover the wall with a soft fabric such as damask. The chosen fabric should closely match the color of the wall paint, so there's an uninterrupted flow between the two areas. To add architectural interest cheaply and quickly, a border print in a complementary pale pattern is applied at

Above, a fabric-covered screen divides this studio apartment neatly into two separate areas: one for relaxing and one for sleeping. Since the screen doesn't extend from floor to ceiling, the two spaces don't seem closed in. Opposite, everything in the bedroom was chosen for softness, from the padded headboard to the damask-covered walls, yet there's nothing too intimate about the space.

To maintain a successful open-floor plan, keep your color palette consistent throughout the space.

chair-rail height. Gold, yellow, and blue are used as accent colors.

In the open bedroom area is a mix of family treasures, flea market finds, and inspired ideas that aren't generally associated with the boudoir. The nightstand, which could also be an end table, is recycled from childhood. Nighttime necessities are tucked inside the drawers. On top are family photos and a miniature dress form that holds necklaces. On the screen, hanging from a gold French wire ribbon, is a baby picture. The padded headboard is reversible—bold stripes on one side (shown here) and a check print on the other. The duvet is made of the same fabrics, to encourage mixing and matching.

The living area is set up to encourage cozy conversation. The pieces are placed on angles toward one another so visitors are always in close proximity. Furnishings are slipcovered in a quiet mix of patterns in similar shades of yellows, whites, and beiges. Nestled between the sofa and the armchair is a table, which can hold guests' drinks or even a dinner plate. The table, hidden beneath a crewelwork cloth, is made of cheap particleboard and is available through home furnishings catalogs. An upholstered ottoman functions as a cocktail table as well as a footrest.

Blue-striped pillows serve as a counterpoint to the neutral color scheme in the living room. One wall of this studio is set aside for a gallery of old black-and-white family photos and travel pictures in a variety of unmatched frames.

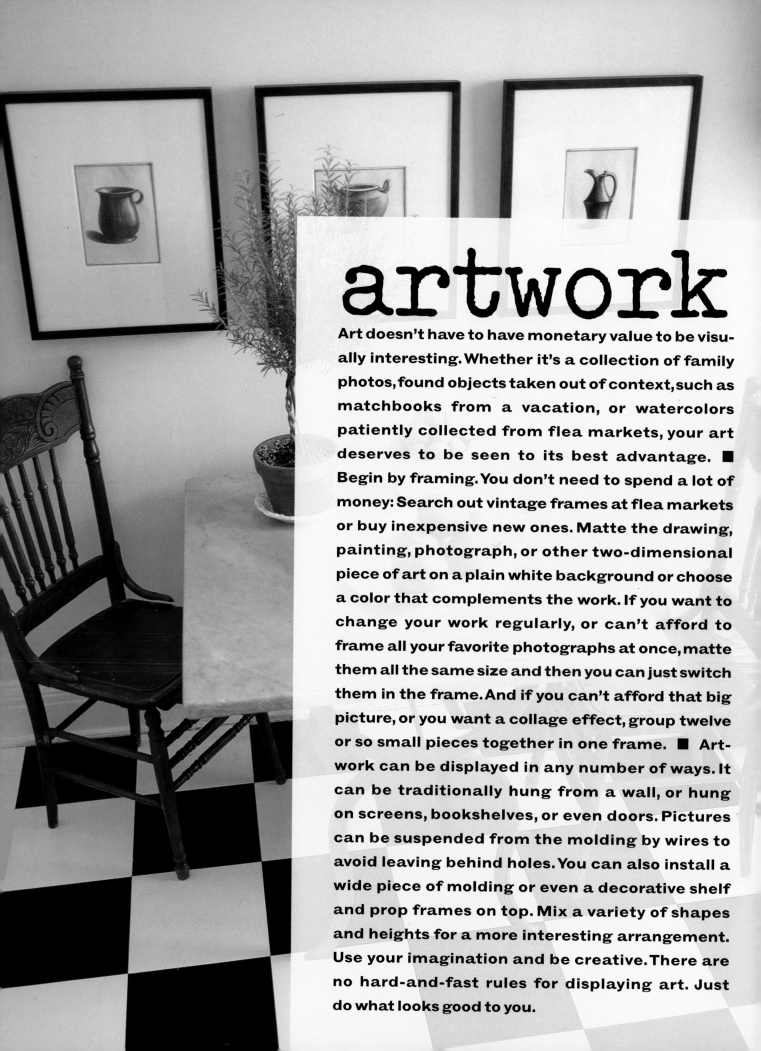

artwork

Art doesn't have to have monetary value to be visually interesting. Whether it's a collection of family photos, found objects taken out of context, such as matchbooks from a vacation, or watercolors patiently collected from flea markets, your art deserves to be seen to its best advantage. ■ Begin by framing. You don't need to spend a lot of money: Search out vintage frames at flea markets or buy inexpensive new ones. Matte the drawing, painting, photograph, or other two-dimensional piece of art on a plain white background or choose a color that complements the work. If you want to change your work regularly, or can't afford to frame all your favorite photographs at once, matte them all the same size and then you can just switch them in the frame. And if you can't afford that big picture, or you want a collage effect, group twelve or so small pieces together in one frame. ■ Artwork can be displayed in any number of ways. It can be traditionally hung from a wall, or hung on screens, bookshelves, or even doors. Pictures can be suspended from the molding by wires to avoid leaving behind holes. You can also install a wide piece of molding or even a decorative shelf and prop frames on top. Mix a variety of shapes and heights for a more interesting arrangement. Use your imagination and be creative. There are no hard-and-fast rules for displaying art. Just do what looks good to you.

Lofty inspirations

This luxurious-looking loft was once part of an industrial building that housed heavy machinery. To make it a more homelike space, color and pattern were generously applied to the room. Painting the window frames and baseboards aqua blue makes the canary yellow walls look even richer—and highlights the beautiful woodwork.

The main living area has two looks—winter and summer—achieved by using slipcovers. In colder months, the sofa, armchair, and ottoman are covered in more saturated colors. When the weather gets warmer, they're replaced with matching slipcovers in seafoam polished cotton.

A space this large is tailor-made for parties. When arranging furniture in your living area, avoid pushing all your furniture up against the wall, leaving a coffee table stranded in the middle. The room will end up looking like a hotel lobby. You want pieces arranged so people can comfortably chat with one another. If you're in doubt, see where your furniture ends up after your next party. Good advice to follow: Place furniture on angles facing one another; scatter lots of small tables throughout the room, set down a rug to define the conversation area, and don't block the natural flow of people through the room with stray pieces of furniture.

The space outside the kitchen is set aside for a formal dining area. A thick velvet

In an open-floor plan, "rooms" should flow effortlessly into one another yet still be closely related. In a corner of this loft, a library ends in a home office hidden behind an opaque glass screen. Comfortable leather chairs, perfect for sitting and reading, are conveniently set up in front of a bookcase. In addition to displaying books, the case acts as an easel for a framed black-and-white photo.

curtain hung in the archway that separates
the two rooms can be closed off to muffle
any cooking noise or hide any mess. Here,
in place of a matching dining set, a polished-
steel table is paired with Chippendale-style
wood chairs. The chairs were painted black
then gold-leafed in a few spots. On the seats
are handkerchief-style skirts, made from
leftover slipcover fabric. A sheer metallic
silk curtain (theatrical scrim is a good, inexpensive option) is hung in front of the window to diffuse strong southern sun. It can
also hide an unattractive view without block-
ing light.

The table is set for a buffet with stacks of
plates, cutlery, linens, and glassware so
guests can serve themselves. Even if you
have a real dining room, you don't have to
devote yourself solely to seated dinner parties. A buffet allows people to choose what
they want and gives them a chance to min-
gle with everyone.

On the far side of the apartment, at the
end of the bookshelves, a glass screen
divides the living room space from the home
office. Most of the space is devoted to an
L-shaped work top, which allows you to set
up your computer and spread out paperwork, too. Files and paperwork are kept out
of sight in cube cabinets with frosted-glass
windows that offer a muted reminder of
what's inside. Glass-front kitchen cabinets
work just as well. One of the benefits of
working at home is that traditional office
decor no longer applies: Note the gilded
frame around the computer screen.

**Above, a glazed wall, a gold metallic sheer tablecloth, and a
pair of candelabra create a dramatic entrance to this loft.
Right, an inexpensive way to add a handcrafted touch to
your windows: Instead of a valance, suspend a garland of
dried herbs, fruits, and flowers wrapped around a gold cord
across the top. You can also hang grapevines, silk flowers,
or wide ribbon.**

Opposite, although the equipment in this home office is high-tech, the accessories have a soft touch: engravings from trips to Venice, fresh plants, personal mementos, and a collection of lusterware sit on top of the cabinets. Experiment with a new look by making slipcovers for your furniture. Don't forget to take into consideration pillows and ottomans, too. The living area in this loft mixes color and pattern in winter (top) yet relies on a single solid shade in summer (above) for dramatically different looks. A symmetrical arrangement is a fun way to show off pairs and can also help organize some of your collectibles. If you like the look, but don't necessarily own matching sets, seek out objects close in scale and subject matter such as the paintings on either side of this handsome wood dresser, above right.

smart tip

If you have great-looking windows and a terrific view, as with these arched windows, and privacy isn't an issue, leave them bare. Drapes will only distract.

Chic comfort

From the moment you walk in the door of this city studio, you feel as if you've been transported to a seaside cottage. And since summer residences are often furnished with a mix of castoffs and comfortably worn furniture, it's easy to duplicate the look on a budget. Summer places are often small, so a studio fills the bill perfectly. Although space is at a premium, separate sleeping, eating, and entertaining areas are arranged.

White is the predominate color here, ranging from pale eggshell to butter. It acts as a neutral background for a garden variety of prints from the thirties and forties. Discovered at flea markets and tag sales, they were once tablecloths, quilts, coverlets, and drapes. Now the fabric is used to cover pillows and furniture, and finished with complementary vintage trim. Parquet floors were given a single coat of creamy white paint to keep things light.

For furnishings, bring the outdoors inside. An old wrought-iron garden table with a glass tabletop works just as well as a coffee table. The dining table and chairs are also a vintage wrought-iron set softened by many summers in the sun. An old wooden bench with peeling paint left intact to preserve its rustic look finds a new use as a book stand at the foot of the bed. Old cupboards can be used to hold dishes or clothes, depending on where you place them in the room. Seascapes and pastoral scenes are obvious art choices for this cozy refuge.

Above, sitting in this serene studio, you would never know that outside is a bustling city, not crashing waves. Keys to a summer house look: white-painted floors, a sisal rug, big floral patterns, and white iron furniture. Vintage fabrics from the forties and fifties are now highly sought after by collectors—and prices have risen in the past few years. Look for frayed or torn pieces (rejected by connoisseurs) and salvage sections to cover pillows and chairs. Opposite, above, don't be discouraged if you don't find enough to upholster large pieces of furniture; notice that the seat cushion is a different pattern than the rest of the chair, and it works just fine. Opposite, below, don't automatically rush to sand and paint old wooden pieces. The naturally worn patina of an old cupboard and footstool is a beautiful reminder of their past. Left, decorative extra pillows on the bed can also be used as floor cushions. The nightstand is a filing drawer that may have been used in a store.

step-by-step
projects

GALLERY SHELF

MATERIALS

¾-by-2-inch piece of plywood
½-by-2-inch piece of plywood
wood glue
1½-inch finishing nails
wood putty
fine sandpaper
primer
white semigloss paint
2-inch metal L-brackets (one for every 3 to 4 feet)
screws appropriate for your wall type

TOOLS

tape measure
handsaw
hammer
nail set
putty knife
level
pencil
screwdriver

Determine the length of each shelf. Cut each piece of wood to the desired length. The ¾-by-2-inch piece of plywood will be the actual shelf. The ½-by-2-inch piece of plywood will be the lip that will hold the pictures on the shelf.

1. Run a bead of glue along one ¾-inch edge, lengthwise, of the ¾-by-2-inch piece of plywood.

2. Press the lip along the glue-covered side of the shelf and nail into place at 10-inch intervals. Sink the nail heads. Fill with wood putty. Sand when dry. Prime and paint with semigloss paint.

3. Attach L-brackets to the underside of the shelf. Using a level, position your shelf and attach to the wall using the appropriate screws for your wall type.

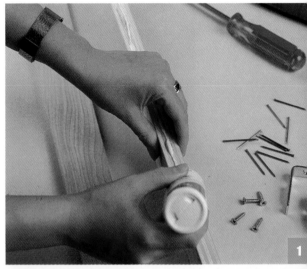

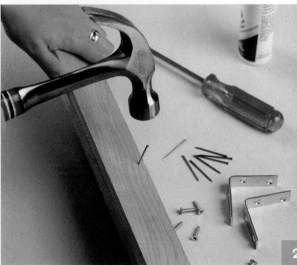

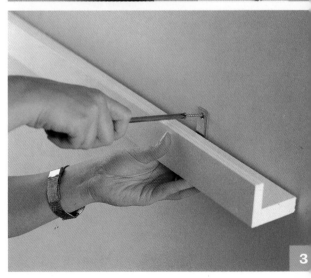

STRIPED LAMPSHADE

MATERIALS
lampshade
acrylic paint

TOOLS
tape measure
pencil
low-stick painter's tape
scissors
foam paintbrush

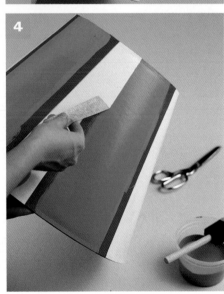 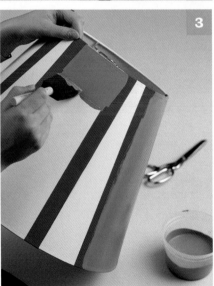

Determine the width and number of your stripes by measuring the top circumference of your shade. Divide the circumference by twice as many stripes as you want. This number will be the width of your stripe. When using a shade that has a large circumference on the bottom, do same to determine the width of your stripes on the bottom.

1. Starting at a similar point on the top and bottom of the shade, start measuring your stripes marking with a straight rule.

2. Tape off each stripe that will be painted.

3. Paint each stripe. Let paint dry.

4. Carefully peel off the tape.

PAINTED BORDER

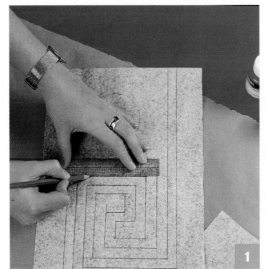

MATERIALS
flat red latex paint
flat linen latex paint
gold metallic paint

TOOLS
graphite tracing paper
straightedge
pencil
2-inch-wide paintbrush
fine artist's paintbrush
small flat bristle brush

Use this Greek keystone and laurel-wreath pattern, or design your own. A good source for inspiration is a book on ornamental design. Determine the size of your pattern by the width of your border. Determine the repeat of your pattern by measuring the length of your wall. Be careful not to let your pattern break in the corner.

1. Draw your pattern onto graphite tracing paper.

2. Paint your background color, in this case red, and let dry.
Transfer your pattern from the graphite tracing paper to the wall using a pencil.

3. Using a flat bristle brush, paint inside the lines of the keystone pattern with the linen paint. You will need at least two coats to cover a deep background color like this red.

4. Using your fine artist's brush, paint the laurel wreaths with the metallic gold paint.

MOSAIC TABLETOP

MATERIALS
piece of plywood cut to size of desired surface
1-inch glass tiles
wood or metal frame (optional)
ceramic tile adhesive
tile grout

TOOLS
pencil
T square
trowel
rubber grout float
sponge

The frame on this mosaic countertop is welded aluminum. You can use a wood frame or even make it without a frame by using the mosaic tiles to cover the edge of the plywood. The fun part of this project is designing your own pattern. This pattern is an interlocking stripe with a border.

1. First lay out your entire tile pattern on a surface the same size as the piece of plywood you will be using for your finished surface. Allow $\frac{1}{8}$ inch between each tile for your grout. This method will help you calculate the amount of tile you will need and allow for easy transfer of your pattern.

2. Apply adhesive to your plywood surface using a trowel, covering only a square foot at a time (otherwise, the adhesive will dry before you have a chance to place the tiles). Working from one end, press each tile into the adhesive securely, leaving $\frac{1}{8}$ inch between each tile. After completing, wait 24 hours for the adhesive to set.

3. Grout the surface according to the instructions on the grout package, using a rubber grout float (squeegee). With a large damp sponge, carefully clean off any remaining grout from the surface.

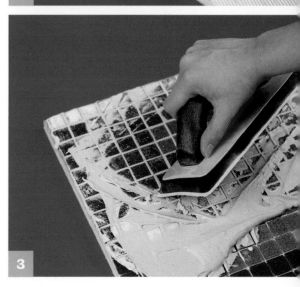

PAINTED WALL STRIPES

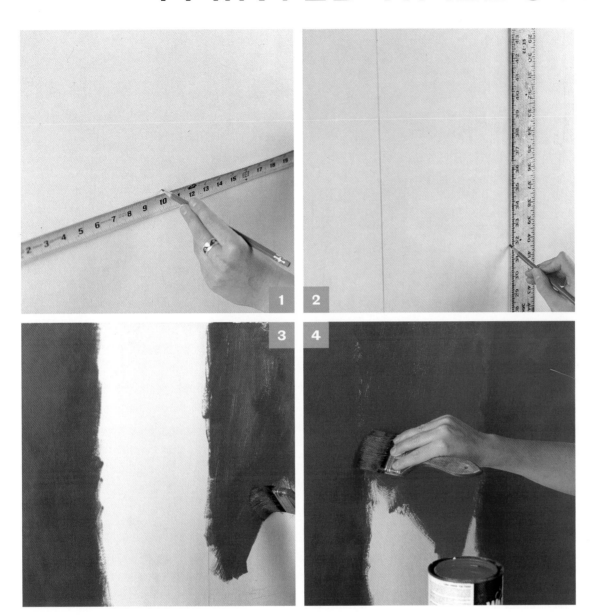

MATERIALS
latex primer
two shades of the same color print

TOOLS
tape measure
pencil
straightedge or plumb line
2-inch paintbrush

1. Prime walls and allow to let dry. Starting from a corner of your room, measure 10-inch-wide stripes, or as wide as desired, along the top and the bottom of the walls.

2. With a straightedge, mark lines lightly with a pencil, or use a plumb line (see page 191, step 5, for description).

3. Paint every other stripe with one shade of paint, using a loose, painterly stroke, keeping to the lines as much as desired (you may tape off the lines for a clean, crisp stripe).

4. Paint the remaining stripes with the other shade of paint, using the same brushstroke. Don't worry about overlapping colors; this only adds to the character of your stripes.

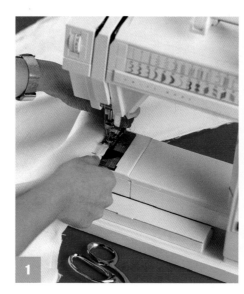

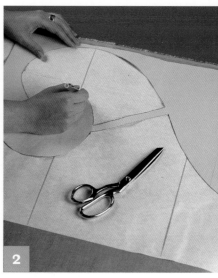

WAVE SHOWER CURTAIN

MATERIALS

3 yards fusing
2⅛ yards blue linen or cotton fabric
4½ yards white linen or cotton fabric
matching blue and white thread
18-by-12-inch piece of cardboard
12 grommets

TOOLS

scissors
tape measure
yardstick
pencil
iron
ironing board
sewing machine
hammer
grommet setting tools

You can adjust the size of the curtain as desired; these measurements are for a standard 72-by-72-inch curtain.

1. Cut two 79-by-40-inch lengths of white fabric. French seam (a finished seam on both sides of the fabric) the 2 pieces along the length of the fabric: Start by facing the wrong sides together. Sew a 1-inch seam along one 79-inch side. Trim the seam to ¼-inch. Fold the fabric back along the stitched edge so that the right sides are facing together. Press. Sew a ¼-inch seam. Press.

2. Draw your wave pattern onto a piece of cardboard. Cut out the pattern. Cut a piece of blue fabric 24 by 74 inches wide. Cut a piece of fusing the same size. Fuse to the wrong side of the blue fabric. Trace your wave pattern, in reverse, onto the fusing paper.

3. Cut out the wave along the top edge of the fabric.

4. Fuse blue fabric (the wave) to the right side of the white fabric by ironing it on. Appliqué the wave to the white fabric using a zigzag stitch along the top edge of the wave. Hem the sides and bottom of the curtain.

5. Fold the top edge of white fabric under ½ inch and iron flat. Fold over again 3 inches, making a 3-inch placket hem, and iron flat. Stitch along the top and bottom of the hem. Following directions on packaging, attach 12 grommets evenly spaced along the top edge of placket. Hang with shower curtain rings.

3

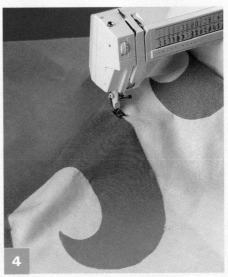

4

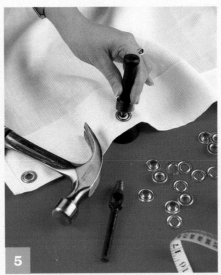

5

PATCHWORK PILLOW

1. Cut out nine 7½-by-7½-inch velvet squares in any colors you want. Cut out a 22-inch-square piece of fabric for the back of the pillow and set aside. Place the small squares together in rows of 3 until you get the color combination you like.

2. Right sides together, using a ½-inch seam, sew together each row of three 7½-by-7½-inch squares. Press the seams flat.

3. Right sides together, using a ½-inch seam, sew the three rows of squares together. Press the seams flat.

4. With right sides together sew the front to the back, leaving a 12-inch opening on one side. Press the seams. Turn inside out.

5. Insert the pillow form inside the case. (I used an Eco-fil pillow form made from Fortrel EcoSpun recycled fibers.) Whipstitch the opening closed.

MATERIALS
fabric
thread
21-inch pillow form

TOOLS
pencil
ruler
scissors
pins
sewing machine
ironing board
needle

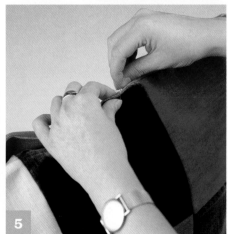

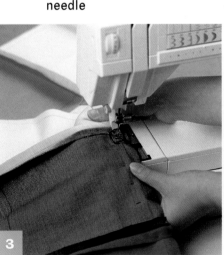

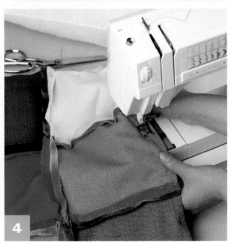

BOX SHELF

MATERIALS

¾-inch plywood
¼-inch plywood
finishing nails
wood glue
proper screws for your wall
2 wood screws
paint

TOOLS

T square
pencil
ruler
handsaw
hammer
drill
paintbrush
screwdriver
level

 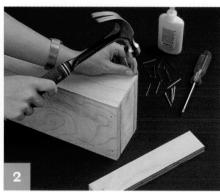 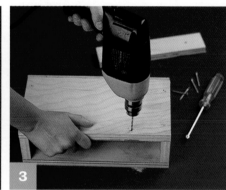

Determine the size of box you want. When combining various sizes on your wall, it's best to keep them all the same depth. You need to determine the size of each piece of wood you will need to make your box. Use this sample size to help you: 10 inches wide by 4 inches high by 5 inches deep. You will need the following size pieces:

¾-INCH PLYWOOD

For the top and bottom: two pieces 10 by 4¾ inches

For the sides: two pieces 5 by 3½ inches

For the mounting bracket: one piece 8½ by 2 inches

¼-INCH PLYWOOD

For the front: one piece 10 by 5 inches

1. After cutting pieces to size, glue and nail the top and bottom pieces to the side pieces, setting the side pieces on the inside of the top and bottom.

2. Glue and nail front piece to sides and top and bottom, covering all the edges.

3. Drill two holes in the top piece approximately ⅜ inch from the back edge and 3 inches in from both sides.

4. Drill two holes in the mounting bracket, centered and 2 inches from the short sides. These will be for the screws that will hold the bracket to the wall. Using the level, find the position on your wall for the shelf. Screw the mounting bracket to the wall using the proper screws for your wall type.

5. Paint the shelf your color of choice.

6. Slip the box shelf over the mounting bracket and screw from the top right into the mounting bracket.

VELVET PICTURE MATTE

MATERIALS
velvet
matte board
white glue
frame

TOOLS
metal L square
matte knife
pencil
scissors

Determine the size of your matte by the inside measurement of your frame. Cut it ¼ inch smaller on each side to allow for the thickness of the velvet. Determine the measurement of the inside opening in relation to the piece of art you are matting. Cut accordingly. Cut your piece of velvet with the width and length each 4 inches longer than the measurement of the outside of your entire matte. Cut the inside opening with the width and length each 2 inches smaller than the opening of the matte.

1. Cover the front of your matte board with a thin coat of glue and center, facedown, on the back side of the velvet. Make sure the velvet is smooth. Clipping the inside corners of the velvet in the center opening, make a cut to the inside corners of the matte opening. Fold the flaps over to the back and attach them with glue.

2. Clip the outside corners of the velvet to the outer corners of the matte. Fold over the flaps, securing them to the back with glue.

3. Frame the velvet-covered matte and art. Secure with a cardboard back.

projects and resources

how-tos

ROUND TABLECLOTH

1. Keep in mind that most fabrics are no wider than 54 inches, so unless you use a flat sheet, you will end up with seams. To keep the seam from ending up in the middle of your tablecloth, panel the fabric so the seams run on the sides.

2. To determine the size of the tablecloth, measure the diameter of the tabletop and add twice the distance from the floor to the tabletop plus 3 inches for the hem. If you want your cloth to puddle on the floor add an additional 4 inches.

3. To determine the yardage needed, add up your measurements for the panel length (the diameter of the prehemmed tablecloth) and then, based on the width of your fabric, determine how many panel widths you will need to create your tablecloth and multiply the panel length by this number. For example: a 96-inch cloth, using 54-inch-wide fabric, needs 2 panels. 96 inches (diameter of cloth) + 3 inches (hem) + 4 inches (puddle) = 103 inches (panel length) × 2 (number of panels widths) = 206 inches (amount of fabric needed in inches) ÷ 36 inches (1 yard) = $5\frac{3}{4}$ yards (amount of fabric needed in yards for a 96-inch-round tablecloth).

4. To sew: Cut fabric into 2 equal lengths, then halve one of the pieces lengthwise. Sew cut pieces to either side of the uncut piece along the selvages (see Fig. 1).

5. Fold the sewn fabric in half, matching the selvage edges and seams. Fold again in half, creating a square. Pin.

6. Determine half the diameter of the cloth ($51\frac{1}{2}$ inches on our example). Cut a piece of string $52\frac{1}{2}$ inches long, tie one end to a piece of chalk (the extra inch goes around the chalk). Pin the free end of the string to the corner where the two folded sides meet, which will end up being the center of your tablecloth. Using the string and chalk as a compass, mark your cutting line in a quarter-circle arc (see Fig. 2).

7. Cut and turn under $\frac{3}{4}$ inches, pin, and press; repeat and hem.

FIG. 1

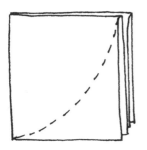

FIG. 2

GLAZE RECIPE AND RAGGING TECHNIQUE

1. Combine equal amounts of clear glaze and mineral spirits, and add enough artist's oil color or oil-based wall paint as you need to achieve the depth of color you want for your walls. Make sure you mix enough to cover your entire room in one batch and test on a white board for color and consistency.

2. Start with a base coat of eggshell-finish paint on your walls a shade or two lighter than the glaze you are using.

3. Immerse a soft lint-free rag (have plenty on hand) into the glaze (use a roller pan for your glaze and gloves to protect your hands) and wring.

4. Bunch up the rag lightly so it has plenty of folds. Dab the wall with the rag to get your desired effect. The harder you dab the heavier the pattern will appear. Step back every once in a while to make sure you're applying the glaze evenly.

TIP For a nice, consistent look this project works best with one person applying the glaze.

STRIAE PAINTING TECHNIQUE

1. Use the recipe on page 179 for the glaze.

2. Start with a base coat on your walls of satin oil-based paint one or two shades lighter than your glaze.

3. Purchase a professional comb, or make your own: Cut V-shaped notches into the straight edge of a plastic lid cut in half; don't worry about the size or shape too much. Or use a piece of corrugated cardboard, exposing the ridges on one side.

4. Use a roller to apply the glaze to the wall, doing one 1-foot-wide section at a time. Using your comb, make one even sweep from top to bottom. After each pass, wipe the excess glaze from the comb. Don't overlap the rows as you go; instead, try to make sure they align evenly. Be careful not to stop in midsweep; otherwise, a mark will show. Work your way around the room. Allow it to dry overnight.

STAMPING

1. Make your own stamps using halved potatoes or erasers (pink gum ones work best). Stick to simple shapes, such as swirls, stars, leaves, diamonds, checks, or numbers. Trace your design onto the surface of a potato or eraser.

2. Using an X-Acto knife, cut out all the negative space around your pattern, going into it approximately $\frac{1}{8}$ inch.

3. Use any type of paint, but for a spectacular finish use metallics. When stamping, don't worry about imperfections; they only add to the handmade quality.

FABRIC WALLS

1. Measure the circumference of your room. Divide this number by the width of your fabric, and determine how many panels you'll need to cover the walls. Cut the panels into appropriate lengths, allowing 4 inches on each panel for shrinkage.

2. Take each panel, one at a time, and thooughly soak in a tub of equal parts water and liquid starch.

3. Starting from a corner of the room, apply the first panel to the wall starting with the top, allowing an extra 2 inches at the top, which you can cut off with an X-Acto knife after it's dry. Work the panel smooth with your hands to make sure no air bubbles are being trapped.

4. Butt your next panel tightly to the first. Don't worry about frayed edges; the starch will bind the threads together. The panels may go over corners; just press the fabric into the corners.

5. This will take up to 1 day to dry. Trim off excess fabric.

TIP For best results use a middle-weight woven fabric in natural fibers such as a cotton or a cotton-linen blend.

WINDOW VALANCE

1. To determine the size of your valance, measure your window width from the outer edge of the molding and add 6 inches to this measurement (you want your valance to extend over the molding). Determine the length by measuring from 2 inches above the window molding down to where you want the valance to end.

2. Transfer a design directly onto ½-inch plywood and cut it out with a jigsaw.

3. To make brackets cut out two 10-inch-by-5-inch pieces of plywood for each valance, or measure the depth of your molding and add 2 inches and use this figure in place of the 5-inch width.

4. Sand and paint pieces before installing.

5. To install: Attach the brackets, long edge against the wall, to the sides of the window molding with screws. Next, attach the valance to the brackets with nails.

6. Sink the nails, fill with wood putty, and touch up the paint.

PADDED HEADBOARD AND SLIPCOVER

1. To make the headboard: Use a jigsaw and cut ¾-inch plywood to your desired shape to fit the size of your bed.

2. Cover the front of the plywood with a double layer of Eco-fil batting, made of Fortrel EcoSpun, allowing the batting to extend over the edges by several inches. Pull the batting around the edges to the back side and staple to the plywood.

3. Cover the batting with a piece of muslin, also stapling it to the back.

4. To make the slipcover: Measure both the front and the back of the headboard, add ½-inch seam allowance to each measurement, and cut two pieces of fabric, one for the front and one for the back.

5. For the gusset (the strip of fabric that runs the top length of the headboard): Measure the length along the sides and top edge of the headboard and then measure the width. Add ½-inch seam allowance to the width along both the front and back sides and add 1 inch on each of the two ends.

6. For the piping: use ready-made or make your own. Have enough to run along the seam of the sides and top for both the front and back panels.

7. Sew the piping along the seam of the sides and top of the front and back panels.

8. Sew the front panel to the gusset matching the seam allowances and then attach the back panel to the gusset in the same manner. Hem along the bottom edge of the slipcover. Slip the cover over the headboard.

TIP For some shapes you will need to insert a zipper or Velcro in the back of the slipcover in order to get it onto the headboard.

RUFFLED CHAIR SKIRT

1. Use muslin, or tracing paper, for your seat cover pattern. Pin to the seat of the chair, marking around the top edge of the seat with a pencil. Add another ½ inch all around for seam. Place your pattern over the desired fabric and cut.

2. To make the skirt, measure the length around the base of the seat taking two separate measurements: first, around the front of the chair from back leg to back leg; second, along the back from leg to leg. Make the width of each piece 3 inches plus ½ inch for seam allowance on the top and bottom (4 inches total), and add 2 inches to the length to allow for the hem on the sides.

3. For the ruffle, use the above length measurements (minus the seam allowances) and double each. Make the width of the pieces 7 inches plus a ½-inch seam allowance on top and 1 inch for the hem on the bottom (8½ inches total). To gather, sew two parallel lines of stitches (set your machine to 4 to 6 stitches per inch and reduce the upper tension on the tension regulator) within the seam allowance. Gently pull the tails of the two bottom threads at one end of the double row of stitches, carefully pushing gathers to center. Do the same at the other end of the fabric until you have nice, even gathers.

4. Pin the ruffle to the top of the skirt, right sides together, and sew the pieces together, keeping the gathers evenly spaced. Finish by hemming the ruffle.

5. Pin the top edge of the skirt to the appropriate sides of the seat cover, matching your seam allowances together. Sew the skirt to the seat cover. Fold in the sides of the top of the skirt and hem.

6. Stitch 2 16-inch pieces of ribbon to the side edges of the skirt top at each of the 2 back corners for your bow-tie closures.

REVERSIBLE PADDED SCREEN

1. Using ¾-inch plywood, cut three screen panels, each measuring 1 foot by 4 feet.

2. To cut fabric for the front of each panel, add 5 inches to the original width and length measurements and cut three fabric panels. For the Eco-fil batting (made of Fortrel EcoSpun), add 2 inches to the original width and length measurements and cut.

3. Lay one fabric panel face-down on a flat surface. Lay your batting on top of the fabric and center it. Finally, position your wood panel on top of the batting.

4. Starting at the center of one edge of the panel, pull the fabric around to the back of the panel and, using a staple gun, staple the fabric to the wood. Repeat this process on the opposite edge and then for the two remaining edges so that you have four staples holding the fabric and batting securely in place. Return to the first edge you stapled, pull the fabric around to the back of the wood, and staple again. Continue this process around the entire edge of the panel, leaving an inch between staples and stopping 2 inches from each corner. Alternate edges to ensure evenness. Repeat steps 3 and 4 for the remaining two panels.

5. To cut fabric for the back of each panel, add 1 inch to the original panel width and length measurements and cut three panels of fabric. Fold each of the edges ½ inch and press.

6. Place the fabric on the back of the panel and staple along the edge of the screen, close to the folded edge, using the same stapling technique as in step 4. Repeat on the remaining two panels.

7. Hot-glue a ribbon or decorative braided trim along the edges of each of the screen panels to cover the staples.

8. Install folding screen hinges 6 inches from the top and bottom corners and attach the three panels.

FLEUR-DE-LIS SCREEN

1. Using ¾-inch plywood, cut three screen panels, each measuring 1½ by 5 feet.

2. To make your fleur-de-lis pattern, take a piece of paper 18 inches wide by 12 inches high and fold it in half so it measures 9 by 12 inches. Draw half of your fleur-de-lis pattern, using the fold of the paper as if it were a seam running down the center of the pattern. Make sure that the pattern spans the full twelve inches in height. (You may want to photocopy a fleur-de-lis pattern and enlarge it to size to guide you.) Cut the pattern out and unfold to yield a whole fleur-de-lis.

3. Trace your pattern onto one end of each of the screen panels and use a jigsaw to cut.

4. Lightly sand all surfaces of the panels in preparation for painting.

5. Paint the panels on both sides, including all edges, with a white latex flat paint, and let them dry thoroughly.

6. Paint each panel, front and back only, in the color of your choice, leaving the ¾-inch edges white. (I used a deep orchid, raspberry, and tangerine here.) Let the paint dry thoroughly. Depending on the color you choose, you may need to apply an additional coat.

7. To attach the panels to one another, lay all three, side by side, on a flat surface. Mark the placement of the hinges with a pencil, approximately 4 inches from the top, where the fleur-de-lis meets the side of the panel, and 10 inches from the bottom. Drill your holes and attach your hinges.

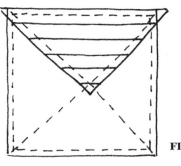

FIG. 1

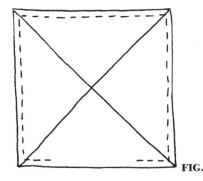

FIG. 2

MITERED PILLOW

1. To make a pattern for an 18-by-18-inch pillow form, on a piece of paper draw a square that measures 17 by 17 inches, and add ½ inch on all four edges for seam allowance. (The pillow form should be slightly larger than the size of the finished pillow in order to create a smoother, more professional-looking pillow.)

2. Pin the paper pattern to a piece of fabric and cut a second square for the back of the pillow.

3. To make the pattern for the front of the pillow, take the original square pattern and fold it twice, into quarters on the diagonal. Cut out one of the four triangles and trace its outline onto another piece of paper, adding a ½-inch seam allowance along the two shorter sides of the triangle. Cut out this piece to use as your pattern (see Fig. 1).

4. Align the longest edge of the triangle pattern to one of the stripes in your fabric, and cut a piece of fabric of the same size as the pattern. Repeat this step three more times.

5. To make your front piece, pin and sew all four triangles together so the stripes align to create a square.

6. Pin the front and back pieces together, with right sides facing each other. Stitch with a ½-inch seam allowance. On one side, begin stitching 2 inches in from the corner, stitch around the pillow, back to the original side, and 2 inches back in from the corner. Leave an opening of 13 inches to insert your pillow form (see Fig. 2).

7. On the diagonal, snip ¼ inch from the corners, without clipping your stitching. Press open the seams and turn the pillow-case inside out.

8. Insert the pillow form and stitch your opening closed, making sure to hide your stitches as you sew.

RUFFLED CHECKERBOARD PILLOW

1. Start with two pieces of solid color fabric (here I used cream and yellow). For a 20-by-20-inch pillow form, cut the following out of one of the pieces: one 19-by-19-inch square, plus a ½-inch seam on all sides; two 8-by-8-inch squares, also with an additional ½-inch seam allowance on all sides. Out of the other piece of fabric cut two 8-by-8-inch squares with an additional ½-inch seam allowance on all sides.

2. To form your checkerboard, select two of the small squares, each a different color, and sew them together on one side. Do the same with the other two small squares. Press the seams open and sew the two rectangles together so that they form a checkerboard square.

3. To determine the amount of fabric you will need for the ruffle, multiply the circumference of the finished pillow by three (which gives you the fullness). In this case, 76 inches × 3 = 228 inches. For a 3-inch-wide finished ruffle, you will need to make the width 7 inches. Therefore, you should cut a piece of fabric that is 228 inches long by 7 inches wide for the ruffle. (If you do not have a full 228-inch piece of fabric to cut, you can piece it together out of smaller lengths.)

4. Fold the ruffle piece in half lengthwise with the right sides facing each other and sew the two short ends together. Press the seams open and turn inside out so that the right sides of the fabric are facing out and press.

5. To gather your ruffle, use a long, loose machine stitch along the lengthwise edge of the fabric. The first row of stitches should be just inside the seam allowance, nearest the raw edge, and the second row should be ¼ inch in from the first. Make sure to leave a length of thread at each end. (Both rows of stitches will be hidden in the seam allowance once the pillow is sewn.) Now gently pull the bobbin threads from either end, working the gathers into the fabric until the ruffle is the correct length to match the circumference of the pillow. Allow 1 extra inch so the two ends of the ruffle overlap (total length = 77 inches).

6. Pin the ruffle to the pillow front, with the right side facing the ruffle, matching your seam allowances (the folded edge of the ruffle should face toward the center of the pillow—see diagram). Sew the two pieces together just inside the seam allowance. Now pin the back piece to the pillow front and ruffle, so the right sides of the back and front face each other and the ruffle is sandwiched between the two pieces. Sew along the ½-inch seam allowance (refer to diagram from Mitered Pillow project). On one side, begin and end 2 inches from two corners to leave an opening large enough to insert the pillow form.

7. Snip ¼ inch from each corner and press open the seams.

8. Insert the pillow form and stitch your opening closed, making sure to hide your stitches as you sew.

HOW TO MEASURE A WINDOW FOR TREATMENTS

1. Whether you are calculating the amount of fabric you'll need for a window treatment or installing Venetian blinds, you will need accurate and complete measurements to ensure a proper fit. Take measurements of every window in your apartment that you are considering a treatment for and keep them handy in a notebook, binder, or file folder along with your other design information. You may even want to take Polaroids of each.

2. Start by sketching your window and wall, including the mullion (window pane dividers) placement, the frame (molding surrounding window), and the windowsill, along with any other details that may be important. Using a metal tape measure, carefully measure the window: the height and width from outside frame to outside frame; the height and width from inside frame to inside frame; the width of the frame; the height of your window from the top of the frame to the floor; and the height of the wall, from the ceiling to the floor (see diagram). Make sure you measure every window in a room. They may appear to be the same size, but often will vary slightly.

3. When measuring for an inside-mounted window blind or shade, always measure the width of the window at the top where the blind will be installed. Sometimes the width at the bottom is slightly different, especially in older buildings that have settled over time.

4. Floor-length draperies should either fall just short of the floor or puddle luxuriously onto it. For puddling, add 4 to 6 inches to your panel length.

5. Curtain rods and brackets usually look best installed above and beyond the window frame.

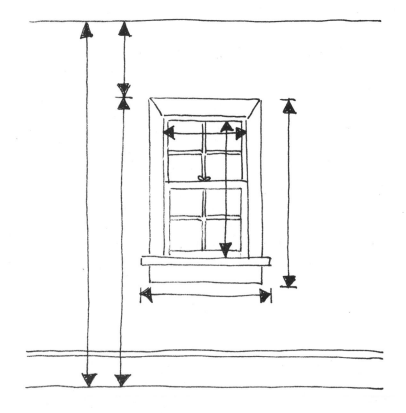

HOW TO WALLPAPER A ROOM

1. Although it is not difficult to wallpaper a room, being well-organized will make all the difference.

2. Paint your molding, doors, windows, and ceilings before you paper a room.

3. Prepare your walls. Remove all existing wallpaper, unless the paper is in excellent condition. Some papers may pull right off the wall, while others will take considerable elbow grease to remove. Renting a steamer may be advisable. If you are papering over a shiny surface such as glossy walls, thoroughly sand walls before washing and sizing. Painted walls need to be washed down. If your wall is darker in color than your wallpaper, you should put up a wallpaper liner or primer first. Next, apply sizing to your walls.

4. Measure the height of your wall from the baseboard to the ceiling in several different spots around the room. Note the maximum height and add 4 inches to this measurement. Hold your wallpaper up to the wall, position your pattern where you like it, add the 4 inches and cut. Cut a second strip, making sure that the pattern will line up with the first, and mark each piece at the top and bottom.

5. To help guide you to hang your paper straight, you will need to mark a plumb line on your wall. Use a professional plumb line or make your own with a piece of string (the length should be at least the height of your ceiling). Attach a washer or weight to one end and cover the string with colored chalk. With a tack or nail, hang the string from the top of your wall at the ceiling, or from the crown molding, with the weight hanging down to the floor. Secure both ends and snap the string against the wall so the chalk leaves a straight line from floor to ceiling.

6. For prepasted wallpaper, soak your paper in a tray of lukewarm water, following the instructions on the roll. Next, pull the paper out of the water onto your worktable. Fold your strip so that the pasted side is inside, make a smaller fold at the top and a larger fold at the bottom. Let the strip sit, or book, for the recommended amount of time to allow the water to soak in and make the paper pliable. For unpasted wallpaper, lay your strip face down on your worktable. Apply adhesive evenly to the paper with a pasting brush, working from the center out to the edges. Then follow the above instructions for folding and booking.

7. To hang the wallpaper, always start in the least noticeable place in the room—behind a door or a spot where the bookshelf is going—just in case the first and last pieces of paper don't line up exactly. Unfold the top section of your wallpaper strip and align it with your plumb line (let it overlap 2 inches at the ceiling). Gently smooth the strip with a brush, working from the center out to the edges, flattening any air pockets. Next, unfold the bottom section, checking the alignment with the plumb line, and repeat above. The unpasted paper will need sponging off with clean water as you go. Trim excess paper at top and bottom with a sharp utility knife.

8. Hang your second strip in the same manner so that the two strips barely touch without overlapping. Use a seam roller to smooth the seams. Continue hanging strips until finished.

TIP Save any leftover wallpaper, or even buy an extra roll if you have none leftover. If your wallpaper becomes damaged at some point, you will have extra on hand to replace it.

HOW TO PAINT A ROOM

1. Before painting a room, you must prep it. If all your surfaces—walls, moldings, ceiling, windows, and doors—are in good shape, then you can simply wash them down with a mild detergent and sponge. If there are cracks or holes anywhere, you will need to fill them with spackle before painting. Apply the spackle with a putty knife until the hole or crack is completely filled. Remove any excess with the putty knife. Let dry. You may need to apply 2 to 3 coats for larger holes and cracks. When thoroughly dry, sand the spackled area with fine sandpaper until smooth. For peeling paint, carefully remove with a putty knife and then fill as above. Wash all surfaces and let dry.

2. Use newspaper, cardboard, or a drop cloth to cover the floor while painting. Tape the covering down to keep it from sliding.

3. Always keep the area you are painting well ventilated. Use a roller to paint large areas such as walls and ceilings. Use a brush for moldings, windows, and doors, and for cutting in (painting a 3-inch band) along the corners and edges of the walls and ceilings.

4. If you are painting the walls and the ceiling, start with the ceiling. Use water-based paints whenever possible, for easier cleanup and less toxic fumes. Paint along the edges of the room with a paintbrush first. Then, using a roller, apply the paint in a criss-cross pattern, overlapping roller strokes for an even finish. Depending on the color and the type of paint you are using, you may need to apply 2 to 3 coats.

5. To paint the walls, start by cutting in around the edges and the corners. Then, using a roller, apply the paint to the walls in a criss-cross pattern, overlapping for an even finish. You may need to apply several coats.

6. To paint woodwork, molding, doors, and windows, use an angled brush. When painting the mullions on windows or French doors, let the paint slightly overlap the glass. (You can remove the paint with a razor blade after it has dried thoroughly.) If you don't have a very steady hand, place a piece of cardboard or use masking tape along the edges of molding and trim.

7. To maintain their longevity, always clean your brushes thoroughly, immediately after you finish painting. If you need to take a short break in the middle of your painting project, wrap your paint-soaked brush in plastic until you're ready to start again.

shopping guide

The following is a list of a wide variety of shopping sources including stores, catalogues, and flea markets, home and abroad.

DEPARTMENT STORES

Habitat
Head Office:
The Heal's Building
196 Tottenham Court Road
London W1P 9LD
0171 255 2545 for catalogue
and mail order
Good for furniture, storage, china, cutlery, linens and rugs. Annual catalogue; 39 branches nationwide.

Heal's
The Heal's Building
196 Tottenham Court Road
London W1P 9LD
0171 636 1666
Everything for the home.

House of Fraser Plc
Head Office: 1 Howick Place
London SW1P 1BH
0171 963 2000
White goods, furniture, bed-linen, entertainment; branches nationwide.

Liberty Plc
Head Office:
210/220 Regent Street
London W1R 6AH
0171 734 1234 for catalogue
and mail order
Elegant and exotic items, stylish accessories; 24 branches nation-wide.

John Lewis
Head Office: 171 Victoria Street
London SW1E 5NN
0171 828 1000
Great for kitchenware, fabrics, furnishings and 'first furniture'; 23 outlets nationwide.

Selfridges
400 Oxford Street
London W1A 1AB
0171 629 1234
Everything for the home.

FIRST FURNITURE STORES

Argos
Head Office
489–499 Avebury Boulevard
Milton Keynes MK9 2NW
01908 600161
Beds, furniture, tools, shelving, storage, etc.

B&Q
Head Office
Portswood House
1 Hampshire Corporate Park
Hants SO53 3YX
01703 256 256
Paints, bathroom products, tiles, garden furniture, wall-paper etc.

Homebase Ltd
Head Office
Beddington House
Railway Approach
Wallington
Surrey SM6 OHB
0181 784 7200
Home improvement products; outlets nationwide.

Ikea
2 Drury Way
North Circular Road
London NW10 OTH
0181 208 5600 for catalogue
Furniture, furnishings and accessories; outlets in London, Warrington, Gateshead and Birmingham.

FURNITURE AND ACCESSORIES

Aero
96 Westbourne Grove
London W2 5RT
0171 221 1950 for catalogue
and mail order
Designer furniture, lighting and stylish accessories.

After Noah
121 Upper Street
London N1 1QP
0171 359 4281 for catalogue
and mail order
Eclectic mix of antique and contemporary furniture and accessories.
Open Mon–Sat 10am–6pm; Sun 12pm–5pm.

Cargo at Carpenter's
Homeshops
01844 261800 for branches, catalogue and mail order
Head Office: JW Carpenter Ltd
Thame Business Park
Thame
Oxfordshire, OX9 3HD
01844 261800
Cookware, tableware, furniture and accessories; 39 outlets, mainly around South of England.

Elephant Ltd
94 Tottenham Court Road
London W1P 9HE
0171 813 2092
Furnishings and accessories; branches in London, Brighton, Bath and Bristol.

General Trading Company
144 Sloane Street
London SW1X 9BL
0171 730 0411 for catalogue
and mail order
China, glass, fabrics; branches in London, Bath and Cirencester.

Graham and Green
7 Elgin Crescent
London W11 2JA
0171 727 4594 for catalogue
and mail order
Furniture, accessories, lighting, fabrics; 4 branches in London.

Grand Illusions
2–4 Crown Road
St Margarets
Twickenham
Middlesex TW1 3EE
0181 744 1046 for catalogue
and mail order
Furniture, accessories, traditional paints, curtain poles, curtains; branches in London, Twickenham and Richmond. Provides one day paint courses.

Green and Pleasant
129 Church Road
London SW13 9HR
0181 741 1539
Furniture, accessories, kitchen and bathroom products, flowers; branches in London and Guildford. Can offer mail order service.

Ikea
2 Drury Way
North Circular Road
London NW10 OTH
0181 208 5600 for catalogue
Furniture, furnishings and accessories; outlets in London, Warrington, Gateshead and Birmingham.

Neal Street East
5 Neal Street
Covent Garden
London WC2H 9PU
0171 240 0135
Furniture and accessories with an Oriental theme. Mail order service.

Purves & Purves
80/81 Tottenham Court Road
London W1P 9HD
0171 580 8223
0171 436 8860 for mail order
and catalogue
British and imported European furniture; lighting, clocks, cookware, storage and accessories.

FURNITURE

The Conran Shop
Michelin House
81 Fulham Road
London SW3 6RD
0171 589 7401
*Designer furniture, lighting,
stylish accessories.*

Ducal Furniture
01264 333666 for stockists and
catalogue
Pine furniture.
Ikea
2 Drury Way
North Circular Road
London
NW10 0TH
0181 208 5600 for other
branches and catalogue
*Furniture, furnishings and
accessories; outlets in London,
Warrington, Gateshead and
Birmingham.*

Indian Ocean
155/163 Balham Hill
London SW12 9DJ
0181 675 4808 for catalogue
  and mail order
*Teak garden furniture, parasols;
branch in Chester also.*

Purves & Purves
80/81 Tottenham Court Road
London W1P 9HD
0171 580 8223 for catalogue
0171 436 8860 for mail order
*British and imported European
furniture.*
Themes and Variations Gallery
231 Westbourne Grove
London W11 2SE
0171 727 5531
*Contemporary furniture,
ceramics and glassware.*

Viaduct Furniture
1–10 Summer's Street
London EC1R 5BD
0171 278 8456
*A range of classical and contem-
porary European furniture and
accessories; also have showroom
in Clerkenwell, London.*

ACCESSORIES

Aero
96 Westbourne Grove
London W2 5RT
0171 221 1950 for catalogue
and mail order
Stylish accessories.

Angelic
6 Neal Street
Covent Garden
London WC2H NLY
0171 240 2114
*Everything relating to candles
and romantic light fittings;
branches throughout London
and in Oxford.*

Appalachia
14a George Street
St Albans
Herts AL3 4ER
01727 836796
Folk art.

Artefact
36 Windmill Street
London W1P 1HF
0171 580 4878
*Decorative interior design
accessories.*

Bombay Duck
16 Malton Road
London W10 5UP
0181 964 8882 for catalogue
and mail order
*Warehouse/showroom for iron
furniture, shelving and accessories.*

David Wainwright
61 Portobello Road
London W11 1LR
0171 727 0707
*Mid–Eastern/Oriental artefacts;
3 branches in London.*

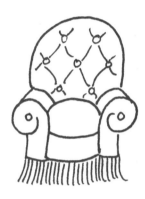

Divertimenti
139 Fulham Road
London SW3 6SD
0171 581 8065 for catalogue
0171 386 9911 for mail order
*Kitchen equipment and table-
ware; 2 branches in London.*

Elephant Ltd
94 Tottenham Court Road
London W1P 9HE
0171 813 2093/2092
*Furnishings and accessories;
branches in London, Brighton,
Bath and Bristol.*

Glassworks
0171 724 0904 for details
Glass products for the home.

Laura Ashley Home
Customer Services
PO Box 19
Newtown
Powys SY16 1DZ
01686 622116 for catalogue and
mail order
*Everything for the home; 165
branches nationwide.*

Mortimers
47 Neal Street
Covent Garden
London WC2 9PJ
0171 240 2900
*Household accessories and
unusual gadgets. Mail order
available.*

Out of the Earth
83 Church Road
London SW13 9HH
0181 563 9991 for mail order
*British handmade contempo-
rary designer furniture, textiles,
ceramics, glass and lighting.*

The Pier
Head Office: 153 Milton Park,
Bromley, Abingdon
01235 821 088
*China, glassware and a wide
range of accessories; 15
branches nationwide.*

Purves & Purves
83 Tottenham Court Road
London W1P 9HD
0171 580 8223 for catalogue
0171 436 8860 for mail order
*British and European contem-
porary designer furniture;
lighting, clocks, cookware,
storage and accessories.*

Staines
15–19 Brewer Street
London W1R 3FL
0171 437 8424 for catalogue
and mail order
*Catering equipment, kitchen-
ware, glassware (including
classic French café–style carafe
and glass sets); 5 branches
nationwide.*

Summerill and Bishop
100 Portland Road
London W11 4LN
0171 221 4566
Kitchenware and accessories.

Wong Singh Jones Ltd
253 Portobello Road
London W11 1LR
0171 792 2001
*A wide range of unusual acces-
sories. Mail order service for
beaded curtains only.*

**FABRICS, WALLCOVERINGS
AND FLOORCOVERINGS**
Christopher Farr
115 Regents Park Road
London NW1 8UR
0171 916 7690
Hand–made rugs.

Ciel Decor
187 New King's Road
London SW6 4SW
0171 731 0444 for catalogue
Fabrics.

Crucial Trading Ltd
Head Office
The Market Hall
Craven Arms
Shropshire SY7 9NY
01588 673666 for catalogue and
mail order
*Fabrics, natural floorcoverings,
rugs and mats; 3 branches in
London.*

Designers Guild
267/271 and 277 Kings Road
London SW3 5EN
0171 351 5775
*Fabrics, wallpaper, furniture;
London and selected retailers
nationwide, including all John
Lewis Partnership Department
Stores.*

Fired Earth Plc
Twyford Mill
Oxford Road
Adderbury
Oxon OX17 3HP
01295 812088 for catalogue and
mail order
*Terracotta and natural stone
tiles, fabrics, rugs, curtain
poles; 16 showrooms nationwide.*

Laura Ashley Home
Customer Services
PO Box 19
Newtown
Powys SY16 1DZ
01686 622 116 for branches
A wide range of home furnishings.

Nina Campbell
at Osborne and Little
304–308 Kings Road
London SW12 8QE
0181 675 2255
Fabrics (also at Harvey Nichols).

Timney Fowler at Selfridges,
Harrods, House of Fraser,
Harvey Nichols
400 Oxford Street
London W1A 1AB
0171 629 1234
Fabrics, floorcoverings and blinds.

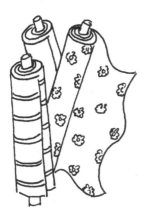

BED AND BATH
Art in Iron
195 Townmead Road
Fulham
London SW6 2QQ
0171 384 3404 for catalogue
Quality iron beds.

Damask Bed Linen
Unit 10, Sulivan Enterprise
Centre
Sulivan Road,
London SW6 3BS
0171 731 3470
Bed coverings.

Early's of Witney Plc
Witney Mill, Witney
Oxfordshire OX8 5EB
01993 703131 for stockists
Household textiles.

Futon Express
56 Chalk Farm Road
London NW1 2QB
0171 284 3764
Futons.

Ikea
2 Drury Way
North Circular
London NW10 OTH
0181 208 5600 for branches
Furniture, furnishings and accessories.

The Iron Bed Company
0171 610 9903 for mail order
Specialists in iron beds.

Kasbah
8 Southampton Street
London WC2E 7HA
0171 240 3538 for catalogue
Tiles, lighting.

Next Interiors
0116 2849424 for branches
0345 100500 for mail order
A wide range of home furnishings.

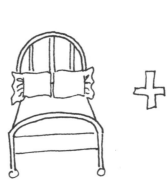 

Ralph Lauren Fabrics and Wall-
papers at Harvey Nichols,
Harrods, House of Fraser and
Selfridges
0171 243 7300 for stockists
Fabrics and wallcoverings.

**WINDOWS, BLINDS AND
SHUTTERS**
Abbott and Boyd
8 Chelsea Harbour
Design Centre
London SW10 OXE
0171 351 9985
or main office: 01737 779 321
Blinds.

The Final Curtain Company
0181 699 3626
Curtains, blinds, etc.

The London Shutter Company
01344 28385 for details
Shutters.

Prêt à Vivre
39–41 Lonsdale Road
London NW6 6RA
0171 328 4500 for catalogue
Ready–to–hang curtains, curtain poles, soft furnishings.

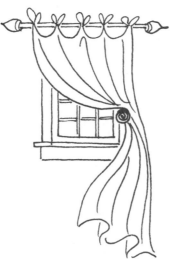

Ruffle and Hook
Florence Works
34½ Florence Street
London N1 2DT
0171 226 0370
*Fabric and curtain
manufacturers.*

Sunway Blinds
0181 906 4277 for stockists in
London and the South East and
catalogue
0161 442 9500 for stockists in
the Midlands and the North
01698 881281 for stockists in
Scotland
Decorative and pleated blinds.

LIGHTING
Angelic
6 Neal Street
London WC2H NLY
0171 240 2114
*Candles, candlesticks, chande-
liers and mirrors with candle
fixtures; 7 branches.*

BHS Lighting
0171 262 3288 for branches
A wide range of lighting.

The Candle Shop
30 The Market
London WC2E 8RE
0171 836 9815
A large selection of candles.

Christopher Wray
Kings Road
London SW6 2YW
0171 736 8434
*Light fittings, lampshades,
specialist lamps.*

Janet Fitch
25a Old Compton Street
London W1V 5PL
0171 287 3789
*Candlesticks made out of
cutlery.*

Junction Eighteen
Bath Road
Warminster
Wiltshire BA12 8PE
01985 847774
*Ethnic candleholders and storm
lanterns.*

London Lighting
135 Fulham Road
London SW3 6RT
0171 589 3612
Lighting.

Mr Light
279 King's Road
London SW3 5EW
0171 352 8398
Lighting.

Sebastiano Barbagallo
15–17 Pembridge Road
London W11 3HG
0171 792 3320
*Ethnic painted wood and metal
candlesticks and holders.*

The Source
Lakeside Retail Park
West Thurrock
EssexRM16 1WN
01708 890253
*Lighting. Also branch in
Southampton: Tel. 01703
336141.*

Space
28 All Saints Road
London W11
0171 229 6533
*Lighting, accessories and
furniture.*

Wax Lyrical
Head Office
4b Swallowfield Way
Hayes
Middlesex UB3 1DQ
0181 561 0235
*Candles. 30 branches
nationwide.*

STORAGE
Aero
96 Westbourne Grove
London W2 5RT
0171 221 1950
Modern, stylish storage.

CubeStore
58 Pembroke Road
London W8 6NX
0181 994 6016
Stackable storage.

Habitat
0645 334433 for branches
Storage and everything for the home.

The Holding Company
245 Kings Road
London SW3 5EL
0171 352 1600 for catalogue
and mail order
Storage.

Millennium
1b–1d Barnes High Street
London SW13 9LB
0181 876 1112
Customized furnishings, accessories; branches in London and Guildford.

Muji
26 Great Marlborough Street
London W1V 1HL
0171 494 1197 for catalogue
Japanese–style storage units and accessories; branches in London and Glasgow.

Oliver Bonas
10 Kensington Church Street
London W8 4ET
0171 368 0035 for catalogue
and mail order
Indonesian and British furniture, and a wide range of unusual accessories; 3 branches in London.

Paperchase
213 Tottenham Court Road
London W1P 9AF
0171 580 8496
Stylish storage.

The Reject Shop
209 Tottenham Court Road
London W1P 9AF
0171 580 2895
Storage and accessories.

Slingsby
01274 721591 for details
Storage.

SEWING PRODUCTS, TRIMS AND RIBBON

John Lewis Haberdashery
Department
A wide selection of haberdashery; 23 branches nationwide.

VV Rouleaux
10 Symons Street
London SW3 2TJ
0171 730 3125
Trimmings, tassels, braids, ribbons.

Wendy Cushing Trimmings at
Harrods
0171 730 1234 X2755
Trimmings.

STUDY FURNITURE AND ELECTRONICS

Argos
Head Office
489–499 Avebury Boulevard
Milton Keynes MK9 2NW
01908 600161 for branches

Bang and Olufsen
186 Kensington High Street
London W8 7RG
0171 937 9444
and other branches
Home entertainment.

Panasonic
Sales and Services
22 Broadway
London SW1H OBH
0171 930 3030
Details of stockists; home entertainment.

Sony
0181 784 1144
Customer Information
Home entertainment.

INTERNATIONAL LISTING

Aero (see **Furniture and Accessories,** *above*)
Outlets in Melbourne, Sydney, Brisbane

Au Bain Marie
8 Rue Boissy d'Anglas
75001 Paris, France
Classic French kitchenware and tableware.

Bed, Bath and Beyond
620 Avenue of the Americas
New York, NY 10011, USA
212 255 3550
A wonderful range of essentials and accessories.

BHV
52 Rue de Rivoli
75004 Paris, France
33 1 42 74 90 00
A wide selection of French hardware and home–improvement products.

Caravane
6 Rue Pavée
75004 Paris, France
33 1 44 61 04 20
Interior design shop owned by designer Françoise Dorget.

Catherine Memmi
32–34 Rue Saint–Sulpice
75006 Paris, France
33 1 44 07 22 28
Designer furniture, lighting and bedding.

Counterpoint
59 Rue de Seine
75006 Paris, France
33 1 40 51 88 98
Colourful fabric and accessories.

Crucial Trading
35 Boulevard Saint Germain
75005 Paris, France
33 1 40 51 05 66
also at:
Hegestrasse 4
20251 Hamburg–Eppendorf
Germany
49 40 480 3707
Natural floorcoverings and rugs.

En Attendant Les Barbares
50 Rue Etienne–Marcel
Paris, France
33 1 42 33 37 87
Animated designer furniture and accessories.

Fired Earth Plc
Nikolaj Plads 11
1067 Copenhagen, Denmark
4533 324422
also at:
Bygdøy Alle 56
0265 Oslo, Norway
4722 436270
Also in Hong Kong
and at:
Chalmersgatun 21
S 41135 Gothenburg, Sweden
4631 167520
Terracotta and natural stone tiles, fabrics, rugs and curtain poles.

Galeries Lafayette
Paris and branches

Hackman Shop Arabiae
25 Pohjoisesplanadi
Helsinki, Finland
358 0/170 055
Finnish–designed tableware.

Illums Bolighus
10 Amagertorv
Copenhagen, Denmark
45 33 14 19 41
Danish modern design—everything for the home.

Marimekko
14 Etelaiesplanadi
Helsinki, Finland
358 0/170 704
Colourful fabrics, bedding, tabletop linens and accessories.

Maison de Famille
29 Rue Saint Sulpice
75006 Paris, France
33 1 40 46 97 47
Classic and country furniture and accessories.

Menojoux
Paris and branches

Museum of Modern Art
44 West 53rd Street
New York NY 10019, USA
212 800 447 MOMA
Modern design.

Tout Ranger
Galerie Le Carrousel Du Louvre
99 Rue Rivoli
75039 Paris, France
42 60 10 85
Modern design.

FLEA MARKETS—AT HOME AND ABROAD

Bermondsey Antiques Market (New Caledonian Market)
London
Nearest tube stations
Borough or London Bridge
Friday 5am to 2pm. Most bargains go before 9am.

Bollate
Piazza Cadorna
Milan, Italy
Sunday 8am to sunset. Italian country furniture, linens and glass.

Camden Lock. London NW1
Saturday and Sunday 9.30am to 6pm. Antiques as well as jewellery, fashions and books.

Camden Passage
Islington
London N1
Wednesday and Saturday. Antiques, deco furniture, glass, lighting and bric-à-brac.

Clignancourt Flea Market
Porte de Clignancourt
Paris, France
Friday to Monday 7am to 7pm. Europe's largest and oldest market; junk to fine antiques.

Columbus Avenue
(at 77th Street)
New York, USA
Sundays all year-round, 10am to 5.30pm. Old and new.

Covent Garden
Tel: 0171 836 9136 Market office for information
Monday 10am to 7pm. Antiques market.
Monday 7am to 3pm. Jubilee Market selling antiques and general bric-à-brac.

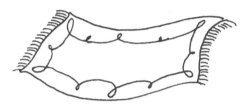

Lambertville Antique Market
River Road
Lambertville, New Jersey, USA
Saturday and Sunday all year-round, 6am to 4pm. Great stuff—low prices.

Lyngby
Copenhagen, Denmark
Sunday 8am to 2pm. Danish furniture and accessories.

Piazza Porta Portese
Rome, Italy
Sunday 9am to 2pm. Mostly small stuff.

Place du Grand Sablon
Brussels, Belgium
Saturday 9am to 6pm and Sunday 9am to 2pm. Fine antiques.

Portobello Road
London W11 1LR
Saturday 5.30am to 3pm. English porcelain, silver, ephemera, furniture, luggage and more. Antiques market at South end. Also look around neighbouring Westbourne Grove and Kensington Church Street for a range of specialist shops dealing in antiques and collectables.

26th Street Flea Market
(at 6th Avenue)
New York, USA
Saturday and Sunday all year-round, 9am to 5pm. Wide assortment of stuff.

Vanves Flea Market
Porte de Vanves
Paris, France
Saturday to Sunday 7am to 7pm. Good buys to be found.

AUCTION HOUSES/ART AND ANTIQUE DEALERS

Chancery Antiques Ltd
357a Upper Street
London N1 OPD
0171 359 9035
Oriental pottery and porcelain.

Christie's (South Kensington) Ltd
85 Old Brompton Road
South Kensington
London SW7 3LD
0171 581 7611
Auction House.

Eskenazi Ltd
10 Clifford Street
London W1X 1RB
0171 493 5464
Lacquerware, screens.

Katie Jones
Stand 126
Gray's Antique Market
58 Davis Street
London W1Y 2LP
0171 493 1261
Baskets.

MND Lewis Antiques
193 Westbourne Grove
London W11 2SB
Ceramics.

Peter W Kemp
174a Kensington Church Street
London W8 4DP
0171 229 2988
Ceramics and works of art.

Phillips Auctioneers and
Valuers
10 Salem Road
London W2 4LD
0171 228 9990
Collectables.

Shirley Day Ltd
91b Jermyn Street
London SW1Y 6JB
0171 839 2804
*Paintings, screens, ceramics,
lacquerware, baskets.*

Sydney L Moss
51 Brook Street
London W1Y 1AU
0171 629 4670
*Works of art, lacquerware,
flower–baskets.*

SPECIAL EFFECTS
The Stencil Shop
Head Office
PO Box 30
Rickmansworth
Herts WD3 5LG
01923 285577 for catalogue and
mail order
*Paints and stencils to decorate
your home; 10 branches nation-
wide.*
*Provides workshops in sten-
cilling, woodgraining and vari-
ous painting techniques.*

Paint Magic Ltd
5 Elgin Crescent
London W11 2JA
0171 792 8012
*Decorative paints; branches in
Arundel, Belfast, London, Sin-
gapore and Calgary.*

Materials and Merchandise Credits

The following is a listing of materials and merchandise featured throughout the book. I would like to thank all of these companies very much for their generous participation in the production of this book.

THE LIVING ROOM

pages 20–21: Toleware by London-Sagalyn, Ltd. Rug and accessories from Inside-Out.

pages 22–25: Josaphine sofa with slipcover by Mitchell Gold. Armchair upholstery fabric, Antique Strie Velvet in Crimson #43050, and parlor chair upholstery fabric, Mohair Velvet, #4000008, in Claret, from Schumacher. Chairs upholstered by Maury Schor, Inc. Traditional Wood Blinds #0032 in Navajo White by Graber. Elfa Easy Hang shelves from The Container Store. Coffee table and aluminum bowls by Patrick Moore.

page 43: Chairskirt fabric, Middleton Linen, #93180 in white, from Schumacher.

page 48: Kathleen Sofa and Paloma Chair by Mitchell Gold. Borneo Lounger by Bauer International. Accessories from IKEA. Pillow forms, Eco-fil made from Fortrel EcoSpun recycled fibers by Carlee Corp.

pages 50–51: Stripe tablecloth, Coloratura in Bordeaux, and cut velvet pillow fabric, Soloce in Burgandy, by Lori Weitzner for Jack Lenor Larson. Accessories from IKEA.

pages 54–55: Sofa throw fabric, Town & Country Velvet #602767 in Claret from Waverly. Curtain panels, twin sheets in Burgandy Stripe from the Luxor Collection by Martex.

pages 56–57: Wallpaper border, Bell Leaf Border #512691 in Sandstone; sofa slipcover fabric, Fern Marseille #57691 in Ivory; fabric framed on wall, Putti #166382 in Charcoal; drapery fabric, Kitami Sheer #15622 in Ivory; all from Schumacher. Throw pillow fabric, Old World Linen #645600 in White and #645606 in Daffodil from Waverly. Pillow forms, Eco-fil made from Fortrel EcoSpun recycled fibers by Carlee Corp. Chair fabric from Gramercy. Ribbon, White Satin, by Offray. Side table from IKEA. Accessories from Wolfman Gold & Good Co.

pages 58–59: Chair and coffee table from IKEA.

THE DINING AREA

pages 66-69: Wallpaper, Aquatio Diamonds #537101 in Offwhite from Gramercy, The Nuance Collection. Wallpaper border, Egg and Dart Border #513200 in Document Ivory; drapery fabric, Middleton Linen #93186 in Linen and #93180 in White; table skirt fabric, Middleton Linen #93186 in Linen; table skirt trimming, Somerset Cut Fringe #892150 in Natural; all from Schumacher. Chandelier from IKEA. Chairs, Sexy Sadie by Mitchell Gold. Iron curtain rod by Graber. Accessories from Wolfman Gold & Good Co.

THE KITCHEN

pages 80–83: Glass Mosaic Tiles by Mosaicos Venecianos de Mexico from Dal-Tile Corp. Traditional Wood Blinds #0055 in Designer White by Graber.

page 89: Fabric wall covering, Country Life in Wedgewood by Waverly.

pages 92–93: Backsplash tiles by Crossville Ceramics. Candelabrum by Patrick Moore.

THE BEDROOM

pages 100–101: Toleware by London-Sagalyn, Ltd.

pages 102–103: Pillows, mattress topper, and comforter filled with Fortrel Microspun Fiberfill by Primaloft. Border painted by Nancy Arner Asch. Duvet fabric, Antique Strie Velvet, Red #43049 and Classic Stripe, Rose #55063; bedskirt fabric, Shenandoah Check, Brick #57163; Roman shade fabric, Classic Stripe, Rose #55063; curtain panels, Middleton Linen, #93180 in White; all from Schumacher. Duvet and bedskirt made by Maury Schor, Inc. Iron curtain rod by Graber.

pages 108–111: Curtain and bed hanging fabric, Middleton Linen #93180 in White, and chair upholstery fabric, Antique Strie Velvet, #43052 in Blue. Curtains and chair upholstered by Maury Schor, Inc.

page 116: Curtain fabric, Town & Country Velvet #602767 in Claret from Waverly. Iron window hardware by Graber.

pages 118–119: Unfinished Shaker table, #8057 by Mastercraft. Iron window hardware by Graber.

pages 120–121: Wallpaper, Magnolia Garden #536422 in Yellow and fabric on duvet underside and buttons, Magnolia Garden #181851 in Yellow from Gramercy, The Astor Terrace Collection. Wallpaper border, Floral Scroll Border #517808 in Red; fabric on headboard, Regent Velvet Stripe #43016 in Red; fabric on duvet, bed skirt, bolster pillow, and sham trim, Atrium Check #91308 in Crimson; fabric on end tables, Middleton Linen #93180; all from Schumacher. Headboard covered in Eco-fil batting made of Fortrel EcoSpun by Carlee Corp. Ribbon by Offray. Accessories from Wolfman Gold & Good Co.

THE BATHROOM

pages 126–128: Porcelain floor tiles by Crossville Ceramics. Walls and mirror frame painted by Thomas Frohnapfel.

page 131: Shower curtain fabric, Middleton Linen, #93180 in White and #93205 in Blue Haze, from Schumacher. Heat-n-Bond Iron-on Adhesive by Therm O Web.

page 133: Wallpaper, Toile Orientale #515045 in Onyx and shower curtain fabric, Toile Orientale #165095 in Onyx from Schumacher. Ribbon trim, Black Grosgrain by Offray. Towels by Martex.

ONE-ROOM LIVING

pages 138–145: Sofa throw, Chenille blanket by Faribo. Desk and bookshelf by Patrick Moore. Wooden curtain rod by Graber.

pages 146–148: Katie Sofa, Tufted Ottoman, and Miles Chair by Mitchell Gold. Padded screen, covered in Eco-fil batting made of Fortrel EcoSpun by Carlee Corp. Padded screen fabric, Roman Damask in Mushroom and round tablecloth fabric, Old World Candlewicking in Linen by Waverly. Pillow on sofa, Bedford Stripe in Wedgewood by Waverly, Home Fashions. Dust ruffle, headboard, and duvet cover, Bedford Stripe in Linen by Waverly, Custom Home Fashions. Accessories from IKEA.

pages 154–155: Pillows by Gayle Spannaus Vintage Pillows.

Apartment Credits

The following is a listing, by page, of participants' apartments:

Anthony Baratta
pages 14–17, 27, 76–77, 116–17.

Gary DiLuca and Melissa Makris
pages 64–65, 94–95, 122–23, 126–28, 151.

Michael Foster
pages 48–51, 60, 71, 114–15.

Anne Foxley and Nicolas Kerno
pages 12, 13, 44–47, 61, 72, 78–79, 110–113, 130–131, 135, 150, 171.

Karen Gallen
pages 11, 38–41, 73, 74, 75, 88, 89, 90, 129.

Robert Gaul
pages 27, 70, 88, 107, 120, 132, 151, 152–57.

Jessica Kimberly
pages 26, 56–59, 118, 168.

Rita London and Eric Schurink
pages 60, 119.

Anne Martin
pages 43, 56–57, 61, 62–63, 66–69, 107, 121, 124–25.

Michele Michael
pages 138–45.

Darcey Miller
pages 8, 12, 34–37, 73, 87, 89, 108–9, 135.

Patrick Moore and Michele Michael
pages 10, 22–25, 73, 80–83, 102–3, 151, 163, 165, 166, 175.

Carlos Mota
pages 28–29, 42, 43, 96–99.

Craig Natiello
pages 31–33, 86, 104–5, 121, 151.

Katie Nelson
pages 91, 106, 146–49.

Laurie Sagalyn
pages 18–21, 84–85, 100–101, 135.

Gayle Spannaus
pages 136–37, 158–59.

Lori Weitzner
pages 27, 54–55, 107, 134.

Katie Workman and Gary Freilich
pages 52–53, 92–93, 172.

index

Accessories
  bathroom, 128, 130
  colorful, 26
  contrasting, 60
  living room, 16, 26, 57, 60
  minimizing, 77
  for ornamental piece, 57
Animal prints, 16, 30
Artwork, 28–33, 40, 49, 55, 133, 150
  See also Objets d'art

Bargains, 49, 50
Bathroom, 126–37
Bedroom, 96–125
  with metal furnishings, 108
  with natural palette, 111
  pillows, 106, 119
  red, 119
  retro, 125
  richly exotic, 114
  royal-style, 103
  in studio, 147–48
  white, 105
Beds, 111, 114, 117, 119, 122, 142,
  147
Biedermeier furniture, 109
Black-and-white photos, 19, 148
Blankets, 141
Books, 99, 134, 142
Borders, 99, 147
  painted, 103, 164–66
Bottles, 52, 57, 72
Box shelf, 174–75
Brassaï (photographer), 85
Budget. *See* Costs
Buffet, 154
Bulletin board, 86

Cabinets
  bargain, 49, 50
  dark wood, 68
  kitchen, 86, 91, 94
  locker as, 103
  in loft, 154
Candelabrum, 94
Candles, 52, 57, 68, 75, 126

Chair
  Chippendale, 44, 46
  Chippendale-style, 154
  fifties dining set, 77
  19th-century spindle-back, 79
  ruffled skirt, 185
  wrought-iron, 158
Chaise, 19, 21
Chartreuse, 16, 44, 117
Checklist, 12
Chic elegance, 63
Chippendale chairs, 44, 46
Closets, 117, 130
Clutter, 77
Color
  in bathroom, 128, 133
  in bedroom, 99, 114, 117, 119,
    122
  in dining area, 68, 71
  in living room, 16, 23–28, 57, 59
  in loft, 153
  in studio, 141, 147, 148
Comfort, 11, 126
Contrasts, 60
Cookbooks, 94
Costs, 9, 10, 80
  See also Bargains
Counter space, 86
Countertop, 82
Cover-ups, 120, 141
Curtains, 52, 57, 103

Daybed, 19
Department stores, 49
Desk, 108, 109
Dimmer switch, 79
Dining area, 66–79
  formal, 68
  in kitchen, 71, 79
  in living room, 34
  in loft, 153–54
  nooks and niches, 71, 75
  patterns, 71, 79
  in studio, 141
Dining sets, 77
Dinner parties, 36
Discount stores, 49, 50

Dishes. *See* Table settings
Drama, 57
Drapes, 49, 59, 68, 122
Duvets, 100, 148

Entertaining, 34, 86
Equipment, 13

Fabric
  in bedroom, 114, 117
  from flea markets, 38, 50
  in kitchen, 91
  for pillows, 106
  in studio, 147
  textured, 16, 52
  vintage, 158, 159
  wall, 182
  for windows, 42
Faucet, 85
Fireplace, 64
Fixtures
  kitchen, 85
  lighting, 91
Flea markets, 23, 38, 44, 50, 103
Fleur-de-lis screen, 187
Floor, 63, 71, 82, 128
Floor plan, 12–13
Flowers, 23, 36, 72
Frames, 64, 79, 142, 150
  See also Mattes
French bistro style, 85
French windows, 19
Function, 10–11
Furniture
  and budget, 10
  living room, 19–21
  recovered, 19
  See also specific furniture, e.g.,
    Table

Galley kitchen, 80, 86
Giveaways, 12, 30
Glaze, 179–80

Hardware, window, 42
Headboard, 117, 122, 125, 148, 184
Home office. *See* Work space

Kitchen, 80–95
  cottage style, 91
  country, 82
  dining area in, 71, 79
  French bistro style, 85
  galley, 80, 86
  hiding, 92
  lighting, 88
  updating fifties, 94
Knobs, 94

Lamps, 88, 103, 142
Lamp shades, 114, 142, 162–63
Le Corbusier, 8
Lighting, 79, 88, 126
  See also Lamps
Linens, 105
Living room, 14–65
  art in, 23, 28–33, 40
  chic, 63
  color in, 16, 23–28, 57, 59
  doubling as dining room, 34
  elegantly eclectic, 38
  glamorous urban, 19
Lofts, 138, 153–57

Mantel, 21, 23, 64
Mattes, 64, 79, 142, 150, 176
Metal furnishings, 108
Mirrors, 30, 75, 105, 111
Mitered pillow, 188
Molding, 133
Mosaic tabletop, 167
Mosaic tile, 82
Moving, 12

Nelson, George, 77
Niches and nooks, 71, 75, 85
Nightstand, 103, 111, 117, 122, 148,
  159

Objets d'art, 23, 28, 55
One-room living space, 138–59
Organization, 11–12
Ottomans, 157

Padded headboard, 184
Padded screen, 186
Paint, 26, 59, 91, 142, 180, 192
Painted border, 164–66
Painted wall stripes, 169
Pantry, 82
Parties, 153
Patchwork pillow, 173

Pattern
  in bathroom, 133
  in bedroom, 114, 117, 122
  in dining area, 68, 71, 79
  on pattern, 50
Personal style. See Style
Pillows, 50, 100, 106, 119, 148, 157,
  159
  mitered, 188
  patchwork, 173
  ruffled checkeroard, 189
Plastic, 77
Postcards, 103
Pottery, 23, 55, 142
Prints, 141

Quilts, 142

Ragging technique, 179
Red, 119
Rentals, and budget, 10, 80
Reupholstery, 19
Reversible screen, 186
Ruffled checkerboard pillow, 189
Ruffled skirt, 185
Rugs, 30, 60

Saarinen, Eero, 77
Screen
  fleur-de-lis, 23, 187
  in loft, 153, 154
  reversible padded, 186
  sliding rice paper, 92
  in studio, 147
Shades, 105
Shams, 100
Sheets, as curtains, 57, 122
Shelving, 142
  bathroom, 130, 134
  box shelf, 174–175
  gallery, 108, 161
  metal, 108, 109
  over sink, 82
Shopping guide, 193
Shower curtain, 128, 130, 133,
  170–71
Sink, 86, 128
Sink handle, 85
Skirt, of chair, 185
Slipcovering, 19, 120, 153, 157, 184
Sofa, 44, 57, 141
Stamping, 181
Stool, 109

Storage
  bathroom, 128, 130, 133, 134–37
  bedroom, 100, 111, 114, 119
  dining area, 71
  kitchen, 94
  living room, 54
Striae painting technique, 180
Stripes, 119, 148, 162–63, 169
Studios, 138–49, 158–59
Style
  of kitchen, 85
  personal, 9, 11, 14

Table
  bedroom, 103, 111, 117, 122
  dining, 66, 75, 77, 79
  folding, 117
  kitchen, 82, 85, 94
  mosaic, 167
  particleboard, 148
  sawhorse, 55
  steel, 154
  wire basket, 46
  wrought-iron, 158
Tablecloth, 178
Table settings, 36, 75
Tag sales, 23
Terra-cotta, 71, 92, 94
Texture, 16
Throws, 120
Tile, 82, 94, 128
Tools, 13
Tradition, 52
Travel, 49

Valances, 57, 119, 183
Vases, 49, 52, 55
Velvet matte, 176
Venetian blinds, 109
Vinyl, 16

Wallpaper, 68, 125, 128, 133, 191
Walls, 141, 169, 179–80, 182
  See also Paint
White, 26, 63, 77, 92, 105, 158
Windows, 42–43, 52
  French, 19
  in loft, 154, 157
  measuring, 190
  oversized, 57
  See also Curtains; Drapes;
    Valances
Work space, 108, 142, 154